R. Worthington

The Canadian brigands

An intensely exciting story of crime in Quebec thirty years ago

R. Worthington

The Canadian brigands
An intensely exciting story of crime in Quebec thirty years ago

ISBN/EAN: 9783741198687

Manufactured in Europe, USA, Canada, Australia, Japa

Cover: Foto ©Andreas Hilbeck / pixelio.de

Manufactured and distributed by brebook publishing software
(www.brebook.com)

R. Worthington

The Canadian brigands

.

LIST OF BOOKS

PUBLISHED AND FOR SALE BY

R. WORTHINGTON, MONTREAL.

JUST PUBLISHED:

Canadian Brigands. A most exciting Story.

Gerald Aymer's Loves, and 10 complete Stories.

A Strange Story.

The Ten of Diamonds, and other Tales.

Long Slippers, and other interesting Tales, by Eminent Authors.

The Hand-Book of Travels, AND TOURIST'S GUIDE THROUGH CANADA AND THE UNITED STATES.

What is This Mystery. By Miss BRADDON.

The Advocate, a Novel by Mr. C. HEAVYSEGE, author of "Jephthah's Daughter," &c., &c., in 1 Vol., 8vo.

The Harp of Canaan, by the Rev. J. DOUGLAS BORTHWICK, in 1 Vol., 12mo., printed on best paper.

History of Canada, by the late ROBERT CHRISTIE, Esq., M. P. P., in 6 Vols., 12mo.

Garneau's History of Canada, in 2 Vols., 8vo., Third Edition.

Artemus Ward, "His travels," with Comic Illustrations.

Artemus Ward, "His Book," with 18 Comic Illustrations.

Hesperus, AND OTHER POEMS, by CHAS. SANGSTERS, in 1 Vol.

Saturday Reader, complete to Sept. 1st, 1867, in 4 Vols., Green Cloth Extra.

Nimmo's Popular Tales, 4 Vols. in 2 half calf.

THE
CANADIAN BRIGANDS!!

AN INTENSELY EXCITING STORY OF CRIME IN QUEBEC,

THIRTY YEARS AGO!!

Montreal:

PUBLISHED BY R. WORTHINGTON.

1867.

CANADIAN BRIGANDS.

CHAPTER I.

DURING the summer and autumn of 1834, the year of the great cholera, Quebec was visited by a scourge, scarcely less alarming than that of the epidemic; theft, assassination and burglary succeeded each other with inconceivable rapidity, carrying fear and consternation into every circle of society; never was crime nor robbery accompanied by more atrocious circumstances, nor committed with greater audacity, in the midst of a moral and comparatively small population.

The doings were no longer confined to the tricks and ordinary sleight of hand of the habitual inmates of the prison; petty larceny, thefts of clothing or of poultry, prompted by misery and committed tremblingly and in secret. They were the attack of an armed band on our public roads, in our country houses, our inhabited dwellings, and in our churches. In vain did the civic authorities institute enquiry and set their runners on foot; the authors of these crimes escaped out of reach and remained undetected. All the known reprobates of the town were questioned, but without effect; not a sign, not a hint, not a guess gave a clue to the mystery; bailiffs, patrols, and magistrates were all of them at a loss; even the promise of large sums of money did not tempt the cupidity of a single accomplice.

The conspirators, secure in their secret, and rendered more and more daring by the repeated failures of the authorities, profited by the fear that paralyzed the citizens, and continued their depredations night after night. Scarcely a day dawned but brought with it the rumor of some fresh attempt; the public journals laid hold of the news with avidity, as a piece of great good fortune, by the horrible details of which they attracted the attention and excited the fear of their readers, who, in terrified suspense, awaited anxiously the unravelling of the plot. Certain it was, however, that if professional thieves knew aught of these misdeeds, a secret hand possessing more than ordinary skill, directed and controlled their movements—the conspiracy or whatever it was, had a *soul*, a chief, far superior to the ordinary run of thieves; a head at once skilful, crafty, and energetic; but where to find this head was the question; the core of the secret had still to be touched; day by day it became more and more necessary to bring the guilty to light, and rid Quebec of the accursed plague.

This state of affairs continued until the spring of 1835, without the discovery of a single culprit, notwithstanding that every precaution had been taken by the citizens, who were always on the alert, and well armed; still thousands of pounds fell into the hands of this audacious band.

Happily the career of crime is not of long duration; the guilty cannot hope for exemption from his deserts; sooner or later his very sense of security betrays him, and delivers him, bound hand and foot, at the tribunal of justice. But a recent and unparalleled robbery gave renewed vigor to the drooping spirits of the constabulary.

During the night of the 9th and 10th of February, 1835, the scoundrels introduced themselves into the chapel of the Congregation of Our Lady, of Quebec; breaking it open they violated this sanctuary, consecrated to the worship of the Virgin, taking away with them lamps, candlesticks, and consecrated vessels, all of which were pure silver, and estimated at a value of from a hundred and fifty to two hundred pounds sterling. So enormous a crime aroused the indignation of the entire population, but, again, as before, time had to elapse without exposing a single trace of the guilty; the vague suspicions that were afloat served only to embarrass the authorities, so contradictory were their statements. One month—two months—three months passed, yet nothing transpired to afford the slightest hope of success; though four hundred dollars had been held out as a reward to the informer, not a clue could be obtained to the secret.

But the guilty cannot remain quiet in their transgressions, and thus avoid their punishment; they are their own informers. The men who, up to this time had eluded all the vigilance of pursuit, were fast weaving the snare that was to entrap them—in their haste to convert their spoils into money—journeying from Quebec to Broughton to have it melted, and despising the caution which had hitherto been their shield, they discovered upon themselves.

An old Irish woman, Cecelia Connor, lived as servant with a man named Norris, a connection of one of the conspirators, in the Township

CANADIAN BRIGANDS.

of Broughton, distant about fifty miles from the City of Quebec. This woman, witnessing an unusual commotion in her master's household—people coming and going at all hours—felt persuaded that something strange was taking place; accordingly she watched every movement of those around her—listened to every sound—questioned all she dared—guessed all she could, and at last, strange to say, questioned rightly; the truth had revealed itself to her—she had fathomed the secret.

One cold winter's night, perceiving a small light twinkling beneath the branches of a distant wood, this old woman, for she was forty years of age, and extremely feeble, actuated by curiosity, arose from her bed and walked towards it, nearly three miles in the dark, and through snow up to her knees; at last she came upon snowshoe tracks—she followed them for about twice the distance of a gun shot—they led to a little hut, used during the maple sugar season as a place for boiling the sap. Creeping cautiously up, she ensconced herself within the shadow of a large maple tree, and awaited in breathless silence, the result of her undertaking.

A man about six foot high acted as sentinel a few paces from the cabin door; he stood upon snowshoes, was armed with a huge and knotty club, and was under orders to fell any living thing that approached. This man the old servant recognised as a brother-in-law of her master's; he had recently arrived from Quebec. The cabin door was partly open, and by the blaze of a large coal fire, she perceived three men, who looked like salamanders surrounded by flames. One of them held a silver figure of the Virgin in his hand, which he was showing to his companions, to whom it appeared to give intense satisfaction, and who were busily employed in tearing off the branches and ornaments from chandeliers and other objects of church service.

Trembling between fear and joy the old woman leaned forward to catch, if possible, the meaning of their gestures, and in the deep stillness of the night the following words were wafted to her ears :

"In the devil's name here's a virgin—chaste is she, and pure—she's the girl to fill our pockets—poor little virgin, from a chapel you are likely to visit many a queer place, let me tell you."

As these words were pronounced, the man who spoke snapped off its arms and threw them into a heated crucible. This person was a lumber merchant of the City of Quebec—his name was Charles Cambray—the two others were Norris, in whose service the old woman was, and Knox, a man in his employ ; he who kept watch without was George Waterworth.

The old woman dared not remain longer where she was, but she had discovered the secret and was satisfied. Enchanted with her success, she hurriedly retraced her steps to the dwelling, and happily she reached it unperceived and in safety. But what could have inspired this poor miserable creature with the thought, the strength, the nerve, to undertake this laborious journey, the discovery of which would most certainly have resulted in her immediate death? Was it not Providence who made use of this feeble instru-

ment to confound those who had baffled an entire population!

Early next morning the four men returned from their night's work ; the servant, in opening the door to them, perceived that Knox was tipsy. She watched her opportunity, and as soon as he had fallen asleep, she searched his person, and found thereon a small silver sceptre which he had stolen from his master, and for several days back had concealed in his shirt bosom. As soon as Cambray and George Waterworth had left for Quebec she went to the magistrate of the place, (Mr. Hall),informed him of what she had seen, and placed the stolen ornament in his possession.

The authorities in Quebec having been informed of these facts, Charles Cambray and George Waterworth, two lumber merchants of that place, both enjoying excellent reputations, were, to the utter astonishment of their fellow-citizens, arrested and thrown into prison.

In the interval, a minute investigation of the particulars took place ; the dwellings inhabited by the prisoners were thoroughly searched, and among the articles found were a telescope and some silver spoons ; these there were good grounds for supposing had been stolen within but a short period of time. From this day, the veil which had hitherto concealed the iniquitous career of the confederacy was torn aside, and they stood before the public gaze in all their nakedness and guilt ; and be it remembered that to a poor weak woman Quebec owed its deliverance from the depredations of this organised band, all the more dangerous from the fact that their position in society and general reputation screened them the more effectually from suspicion.

In the month of September, 1835, Cambray was accused of house-breaking and robbery, committed against a Mr. Parke, who identified the telescope found at the prisoner's, as belonging to him, and in the month of March following, 1836, he was again accused, this time of a most heartless murder committed at Lotbinière on the person of a Captain Sivrac. Owing, however, to the skill of his legal adviser, to the absence of sufficient proof, and to the perjuries of his accomplices, who were unknowingly permitted to give evidence on his behalf, and who came on purpose to prove an *alibi*, he escaped conviction in both these cases.

With regard to the sacrilegious theft on the chapel of " La Congregation," the Attorney-General did not like risking an immediate action,persuaded that time would indubitably bring forth more incontestable proof than that furnished by Cecelia Connor. It was owing to that, at the close of the Criminal Term for March, 1836, Cambray and Waterworth were set at liberty upon giving bail.

In the following August fresh suspicions fell upon them for the theft of building material, and they were again incarcerated.

During the September Term the press of business excluded once more the action of *La Congregation*, and actuated by a spirit of folly, a weakness, an inexplicable contradiction in the character of a man so full of energy and determination, that is if we are not to attribute it to a blindness inseparable from the circumstances to be hereinafter explained, Cambray offered the officer of the Crown to turn King's evidence, and, on certain conditions to give all the details of the crime of which he and his accomplice stood accused. This intelligence reached Waterworth, who, having to choose between death or treason, chose treason, and he also offered to reveal without any condition save that which the law allowed, namely : the hope of pardon and liberty after the conviction of the offenders, all the particulars connected with the aforesaid crimes. This offer was accepted, and the accused remained in prison until the month of March, 1837, when the criminal accusations: burglary at Mrs. Montgomery's, and the robbery connected with the chapel of *La Congregation* were brought on for trial by the frightful revelations of Waterworth, and which finally led to the conviction of Cambray, Mathieu, and Gagnon. Never did criminal trial produce a greater sensation in the public mind, owing partly to the sad celebrity of the prisoners, and partly to the gravity of their offences. During the whole of the March term, 1837, the court was positively crammed with spectators, and the columns of the public prints teemed with the details of the case.

To the number of interesting facts brought to light in the course of his trial are added the still more extraordinary disclosures of the accomplice witness, together with those of the convicted, from whom the material of these memoirs has been derived.

CHAPTER II.

Defectiveness of the Penal Code—Revelations of Waterworth—Appearance and character of W.—First interview between W. and Cambray—An expedition—A frolic.

The voice of crime raised only to gratify an idle curiosity, may inspire the mind with horror, but it debases its purity and corrupts its nature, for it familiarizes it with the path of vice. But when it appeals to the Legislature on behalf of unfortunate fellow creatures, cast by their laws on the highway of crime ; when in the name of humanity it presses upon the consideration of the country questions deeply affecting its honor and prosperity, when it seeks to elevate wretches above their violent passions and sinful dispositions, it then becomes the province of the philanthropist and the patriot, and it is to these effects we now unfold the fearful annals of bloodshed and wickedness.

It is far from our idea to apologize for scoundrelism, nor do we wish to quiet public indignation at an outrage committed against the rights of society. We heartily desire that the guilty may not escape punishment, but we also desire that the law of the land may not have the effect of increasing their numbers, and of compelling them to continue in their misdeeds.

Ask a criminal, a man from whose contact we shrink with horror, ask him the history of his life—he answers, *poverty, weakness*—the error of one moment led to the theft of a loaf of bread, or an old garment—the law laid hold of me—disgraced me with public exposure—cast me into prison among a number of old delinquents, men who glorifying in vice, encouraged the committal of crime. And now, though defamed and shunned by every one, I must still live, and I can only live by crime.

And when this man arrives at the climax of his career—the gallows—when he is brought face to face with death—when at last reflection forces itself upon his mind, and the feelings common to human nature return, writhing in mental agony—bemoaning his bitter fate—kneeling in prayer upon his miserable pallet of straw, deploring his crimes and invoking the mercy of God, for that of man has been denied him—who, without pity can witness the utter wretchedness of his condition, or turn unmoved from so sad a scene ?

Taking into consideration the population of our country, there are few places in the world containing a greater number of criminals ; and to the causes we have mentioned is this frightful progress of vice to be attributed, namely : the defectiveness of the penal code—public punishment—a pernicious prison discipline, and the want of a penitentiary, and houses of refuge to reform the convicted.*

In the present state of affairs, when a man has the misfortune to fall into our prisons, he is lost to virtue ; there the barrier between the first step and the last is removed, the road to vice is levelled by this single act, for the best of inclinations fall amidst the surrounding corruption.

It was to expose this, to point out the allurements that here beset the novice, that we have undertaken to edit these memoirs, for, to detail their importance, whether moral or political, is far above our efforts ; all that we can hope for is, to make the radical defect of our criminal laws felt ; if we succeed in this, we shall be satisfied.

" Yes," said Waterworth, " I desire to enter fully into the details of our crimes, for I now see where this life was leading me to, and I desire from my heart to abandon it. Moreover, I owe society a reparation for having so cruelly outraged its laws. I will therefore speak freely and truthfully ; concealing nothing that may be necessary to a just comprehension of the workings of the confederacy ; after that I intend leaving the country for ever, for my days would be uncertain were I to remain.

" I must acknowledge that it is with deep regret that I bear witness against one to whom I have been bound by the ties of a firm but fatal attachment, but we were leagued for crime ; and conscience, which speaks sooner or later, acquits me of the guilty oath ; still, as the rapid and extraordinary adventures of the past sweep over my brain, from the first offence to the last, I must own that I proceed with pain.

" To me life has been as a dream—a strange fatality—the fulfilment of a dreadful curse. I know not what charm led me to adopt my peril-

---

* It must be borne in mind that this narrative was written thirty years ago. Many of the evils here enumerated, have been to some extent remedied, but it is still to be regretted that but slight provisions are made in our jails for the separation of criminals into classes. The youth incarcerated for his first offence, is compelled to mingle with men hardened in crime, and in consequence, becomes too frequently like them—hopelessly vicious.   ED. S. R.

ous calling, nor what hand pushed me so far. I cannot help thinking that fate presides over our actions, for up to the present moment I have had no idea of the enormity of the crimes I have committed. It seemed to me that every thing took place suddenly and without giving me time for reflection.

"It is with difficulty that I recover from my astonishment at the end of this strange blindness."

"Well! well! I cannot say what power my companion (Cambray) had acquired over me, but one thing is certain, namely : that I would have attempted any thing in the world he might have desired me."

"What! did you say he possessed an influence over you?"

"Influence! Ah, more than it is possible to imagine. I have loved him more than a father, more than a brother, more than it is possible for me to love any one again. There is nothing I would not have done to have pleased him; indeed so much so, that I could hardly believe myself not under the influence of a charm—some magical power. Each time he was arrested I ran and delivered myself voluntarily into the hands of the police, resolved to share his fate whatever the result. Even to-day when my deposition places a halter round his neck—for I am determined to tell the truth—even to-day, I would submit to twenty years exile in the most desolate region on the face of the globe, if I could obtain a commutation of his sentence."

The accomplice witness pronounced these words in accents of sincere affliction, his eyes filling with tears as he spoke, after which he remained silent for several minutes, his spirit prostrate under violent emotion and hideous reminiscence.

George Waterworth is something more than thirty years of age, about six feet high, and well formed. The repulsive manner generally attributed to persons of his class is not perceptible in him; on the contrary his appearance is extremely favourable. He has a remarkably fine head, light hair, regular features, is quick in his movements, in his manner cold, firm, and severe; he has a very large mouth, high cheek bones, and appears very intelligent. But he looks like a man broken by a sudden and violent reverse of fortune; pale, reserved and melancholy, he seems completely subdued by the pressure of circumstances. He has a prodigious memory, but, having heard his confessions, we doubt whether he was courageous under difficulty, or inflexible in his purpose; on the contrary we are inclined to think he was easily led and won over to the opinions of others, though he certainly wanted neither tact nor observation. at least in judging of the dispositions of his former associates. In his religious belief he is a Fatalist, as are nearly all the greatest rogues; in his apparel he carries not the livery of vice and misery, for he is rather neat in his person, and respectably clad.

"Certes the hour advances," observed Waterworth, starting from his reverie and pulling out a handsome silver watch. "This watch," said he, "is all that remains of that trade." But to business. If you are ready to listen, I am ready to tell." And thus he commenced his story :

"I am a native of the county of——, in Ireland, but my family came originally from Liverpool. I emigrated to Canada with my parents, fourteen years ago, and lived with them upon a farm on the Little River road, two miles from Quebec, which place we left several years after, to settle in the township of Broughton.

"I am pretty well educated, as up to the age of thirteen, I was kept constantly at school ;— at present I am something more than twenty-nine years of age. Whatever may be the crimes of which I am this day accused, or which I may avow, I solemnly declare that in my youth I never felt the least inclination to commit theft ; and that before the year 1833, I had never been guilty of an offence of that nature. When a child my disposition was such, that I was cited as a model to my companions. Well, well! I have changed greatly since that time, owing to a combination of circumstances of which I do not know that I was master.

"In the summer of 1833, it so happened that I had to go to Quebec, in charge of some saw-logs belonging to a merchant of that place; one day whilst in port, a man of pretty good appearance jumped from the shore, upon the raft on which I was, and in a very abrupt manner accosted me as follows :"

"'Boy,' said he, 'you've some pretty good wood there ; come, let's strike a bargain ; what's your price ?'"

"'This wood is not for sale, sir,' said I ; 'it does not belong to me, but to my master.'"

"'Bosh. What does that matter? nobody need know : come, make up your mind ; I'll give the money for it, cash down ; it will line your purse and make a man of you. Here, I'll give you so much a foot (mentioning the price) ; come, don't be a child.'"

"'Oh no, no ; I shall consent to nothing of the kind.'"

"'Well, good-bye, my boy ; I hope your scruples will pass away by the time you're in business for yourself.' However, since you won't sell, at least if you happen to find any thing, just bring it along to me. I'll give you a good price, never fear—and I say, send your friends to me too. By the bye, you don't know me ; my name is Charles Cambray, I'm a dealer in wood ; my place of business is in the Palais ; you'll always find me there : come on shore sometimes and have a glass of punch with me.'

"I accepted his offer, and thus terminated my first interview with this man. From that day we became more and more intimate—the remainder is known to you all

"But to continue ; from that time I acted upon the suggestions he had thrown out, being constantly on the look out for drift wood which I collected in considerable quantities and sold to him. In a short space of time I had amassed much more money than I had ever possessed in my life, and my ideas extending with my appreciation of the business, I soon learned the method of extracting logs from the booms around me, a most lucrative occupation which I followed, I must confess, without the slightest remorse, for I could not then foresee the end to which it was leading me. Nevertheless it must be admitted that queer notions exist in Canada concerning

CANADIAN BRIGANDS.

5

individual rights in lumber, for the entire trade
is little else than pillage from the very beginning;
many a man scrupulously honest in the ordinary
affairs of life is a perfect Turk in this.

"Shortly after the close of the navigation, and
just as I was on the point of returning to
Broughton, I happened accidentally to meet
with Cambray, who, addressing me in an in-
sinuating and persuasive manner peculiarly his
own, said—

"'Waterworth, my brave fellow, you're the
very man I wanted to see. A word in your ear;
I know where there is some splendid wood to be
had at a distance of only some nine or ten miles
from Quebec. What do you say to it? I can
assure you there's a good haul to be made; one
night tide and the profit is our own.'

"We undertook the expedition with the happiest results; we brought back about ten pounds
worth of wood, for which I received ten shillings
as my share. On our return, Cambray said to
me:

"'George, I know you to be a wide-awake fellow, and up to business. Now leave Broughton
early next spring, and I will give you an interest
in my business. You'll see how we'll get on together. But before you go, I've a little trick to
propose. You know that in our trade we'll want
a boat; she must be a first-rate one, a genuine
skimmer, now your brother-in-law, Norris, has
the very thing we want; he'd sell I know, but
then he'd ask such a d—— of a price; but what
I want to know is, what's to prevent you hook-
ing it?

"'What! would you have me act in that way
towards one who has supported me during a
whole summer? I think that would hardly be
the thing.'

"'Tut, tut, deuce take it, it would be charit-
able at any rate, for it would keep him from
stealing wood.'

"'Come now, no folly; give me your hand;
there it's agreed. I'll go with you myself; just
you get hold of the key, and see if the boat don't
vanish.'

"The next day Norris' boat was snug in winter
quarters, in Black Jack's yard, St. Rochs, but it
was not Norris who put it there.

"After this little frolic, as we called it, I can
scarcely say I looked forward to my partnership
with any great pleasure, for I could not forget
that it would be with a man who had taught me
to steal, stolen with me, and finally stolen from
me; in fact I gave him to understand that I did
not think I could accept his offer, and even went
so far as to claim my share in the boat. He
then gave me a note for five dollars; our prize
was worth forty at least, and shortly afterwards
I left for Broughton, by no means satisfied with
the result.

"At this time Cambray appeared to be doing
a good business, he had always plenty of money,
and lived exceedingly well. He was very
regular in his habits excepting indeed the morning after a gale of wind, when he was always up
at day-break. He had also a desperate passion
for cock fighting.

"He was not married at that time, and boarded
at the house of one of his friends. I do not
think that he was then on familiar terms with

the inmates of the prison, nor do I believe he ever
did any thing worse than find, but then it must
be remembered that he found a tremendous lot.

"I did not however like the appearance of
those he employed on his rafts; they were the
veriest scum of vagabonds picked up on the
plains of Abraham, who all of them possessed a
terrible propensity for finding gloves, handkerchiefs, coats, and in fact every thing that could
be eclipsed in their hats or pea jackets.

CHAPTER III.

Cambray and Waterworth enter into Partnership—
Appearance and character of Cambray—A me-
thod of gaining at raffles—The lumber trade—The
Skimmers—The Lion's share—Cambray marries—
His wife—His father.

"I remained the winter at my father's in Broughton, and early in the spring, 1834, I returned to
Quebec, where I saw Cambray, who again urged
me to enter into partnership with him, a proceeding I finally adopted, though not without
much hesitation.

"One day he announced to me that he had hired a house in St. Rochs, where we both took up
our quarters on the first day of May. He also
informed me about the same time that he was engaged to a young Canadian girl, of whom he said
he was greatly enamoured.

"Cambray at that time lived well, spent a good
deal of money, speculated largely, and was, generally speaking, looked up to by the class of people with whom he associated, who were surprised that a young man commencing business could
find so much money and meet with such great
success. The consequence was, that he had
many friends, and was visited and esteemed by
the most respectable of people.

"Cambray is about my age, much more robust
in figure, but scarcely as tall. He has a well-
shaped head, regular features, is strongly set,
broad shouldered, easy in gait, engaging in manner, light-hearted, and pleasing in his address,
that is, when his object is to entrap or deceive
you. But when agitated by his violent passions,
when plotting a conspiracy, when seeking rather
to overthrow than avoid the obstacles that may
intervene between him and his purpose, his appearance becomes totally changed. His habitual mask of hypocrisy falls, and you have before you a frightful spectre; his eyes sink into
his head, and sparkle with hellish fire; his forehead becomes seamed with wrinkles, and the
muscles of his face twitch so violently that they
seem almost ready to snap asunder. His half-
opened mouth moves convulsively from side to
side, his thin lips become livid and quivering,
and his teeth gnash most fearfully.

"This picture may appear overdrawn to those
who have not seen this man under the influence
of his evil nature, but not to those who have
watched the rising fury of his heart; not to
those who have seen him whispering his dreams
of blood into the ear of a hired assassin—wrapped in the mysteries of a conspiracy, or executing
his evil deeds by the glimmer of a dark lantern.
These can affirm the truth of my statements; and
let those who doubt, visit him within the walls
of his prison where he can have no possible in-

terest in misleading them, and there speak the convictions of the moment.

"But the most powerful, I might almost say the only passion of this man, that on which all others are based, in which all his feelings centre, the great lever of his every thought and action, is the love of gain—the desire of acquiring wealth—coveteousness—the ambition of becoming rich. This is the leading trait in his character; to this he owes all the hypocrisy and deceit of his career. But among other peculiarities we might reckon, his astonishing success in games of activity—his jovial humour—his incessant babbling—his imperious bearing—his absolute indifference to the feelings of others—his powerful will and resolute courage. Indeed, were it not for the unmanly vice of hypocrisy, he possesses many noble attributes, for generally speaking, his actions were conducted on a large scale; his enterprises being extensive and hazardous.

"I must avow, however, that I cannot speak of him with impartiality, so great has been his power over me. Still, it must not be supposed that he was addicted to the low and shameful vices of the vulgar; on the contrary his manners were far from dissolute, and never in the course of my intimacy with him, have I seen him in a state of intoxication. He was deeply attached to gambling, and games requiring manual dexterity, and he was remorseless in the exercise of the art of juggling, in which he was thoroughly versed.

"After my arrival from Broughton, I know that he several times attempted to entrap his friends, among whom were some of the most respectable citizens of St. Rochs, and to such an extent did he carry it, that many began to suspect that he was not strictly honourable in his dealings.

"On one occasion, when preparing to move into the house he had hired in St. Rochs, he held a raffle of certain effects, for which he said he had no use, and which, in value, he said, amounted to about fifteen or twenty pounds. At his raffle he had the luck to win back almost everything. This will not however, appear very extraordinary when the reader is informed that he made use of loaded dice, a practice he pursued with such rare dexterity, that he could glide the dice in or out of the boxes as rapidly as he pleased. Several of his companions present at the time, appeared to place but little belief in such strange good luck, and could not help murmuring in an under tone, but none of them attempted to give public expression to their sentiments, for it was dangerous to question the probity of a man whom the community at large held in such high respect. But when his dupes had left, his father reproached him sharply for his trickery, and for holding a course which could only terminate in shame and infamy. On this occasion the old man spoke as if he had had other proofs of his son's speculations. This did not seem to have been the first lecture he had received on the chapter of honesty.

"On the opening of the navigation we commenced the lumber trade in partnership, and on a rather extensive scale for us. To recount all the tricks, frauds, smugglings, doings, jobs and bargains we had recourse to during that summer, would take up far too much of our time; suffice it to say that scarcely a night passed

without our securing a good haul of wood. One of our practices was to cut, at high tide, the fastenings of the cribs with which vessels are loaded, and await the result some distance below; as the tide descended, our booty descended with it, and always found us ready for its reception.

"Another portion of our operations consisted in bribing the guides of the large rafts, from Upper Canada, who gave us their masters' goods at a very low valuation. Again we had a number of *skimmers*, as they were called, of which L—— was chief; they visited the coasts after stormy weather. Then we employed a gang of labourers, whose duty consisted in effacing the various brands from the wood which fell into our possession.

"This dangerous traffic often failed to be profitable, and gave us a great deal of trouble; many came to inquire after lost property, and to claim what they considered to be theirs. In such cases, however, the effrontery and brusque manner of Cambray always succeeded in diverting them from their purpose, glad to be quit of him at any cost.

"I remember that one week we sold the same lot of wood three times over, and twice to the same individual. It is true, we had considerable opposition in this line of business, but with this exception, things went very smoothly. I have no doubt that, at the end of the season, our profits were large; but of this I cannot speak with certainty, having received but a very small portion.

"My partner, perceiving my love for pleasure and dissipation, and my inclination to indulge in drink, very wisely observed that it would be more to my advantage to leave my entire gains in his hands till the termination of the fall business, when I could receive the whole amount at once. This I allowed myself to be persuaded into, and from that moment Cambray kept the accounts of the firm altogether in his own hands. When the time came to render me an account of the same, all the books had disappeared, and by way of a statement, I had to content myself with an illegible scrawl, together with the good round sum of two pounds. Previous to this I had received five pounds, so that it turned out that I had risked my reputation, and in many instances my life, during a whole summer, for the sum of seven pounds. However, I had to put up with it, for to have reasoned with him would have been madness.

"In the course of that summer Cambray made several gains in cock-fighting, but he also lost more than he gained. One day, disconcerted with a recent loss, he said to me, "Why am I such a fool as to continue betting in this manner—why cannot I content myself with the dice-box—game cocks are not *plumped* as easy as dice—it will take many a good throw to make up for my losses. To avoid the necessity of paying these losses in future, he transferred his effects to me, that is until he married, when he made over everything to his wife.

"His wife was young, respectably connected, mild, amiable, honest, and loved her husband to distraction, but she sought rather too much to acquire an influence over him. It was astonishing that this man, so imperious and so violent towards others, yielded with such good grace to her every caprice, and indeed almost allowed himself to be guided by her. Still, I thought he was not perfectly sincere in his submission; that a great part of it was only feigned, the better to conceal his real character. Be this as it may, she was certainly mistress in the house; out of it, however, he indulged in tricks on which her opinion would certainly have been received with very little favour. One day having taunted him on his amiable weakness, he coolly replied: 'If I find her troublesome, I know a remedy.' They appeared to live very contented, but he did not act with the same courtesy towards his father; at times even going so far as to administer slight corporal punishment, when the good man, who was rather given to moralize, touched too acutely upon the foibles of his son.

CHAPTER IV.

Mrs. A——A dialogue—An expedition to the Island of Orleans—Two blunders—Burglary at Mr. Atkinson's.

"To my misfortune I once knew a Mrs. A—— Her husband, with whom I had been intimate, had been dead several years. This woman kept a little tavern in the St. Lewis suburbs, where I occasionally resorted to pass an evening, and here it was I first contracted those connections which have since led to my ruin.

"One evening, having remained much later than usual, as I lay upon the counter, quietly puffing my pipe, I heard the following dialogue proceed from a small room adjoining.

"'Deuce take it, we got off nicely—those cursed butchers never sleep a wink the whole night. As soon as I saw the light I jumped ten feet good off the ground, and hurt my leg most awfully; and look here, look at this for a piece of meat, and say whether it was worth while risking one's whistle for a filthy end of brisket.

"'Ah yes, our trade is done for in town; the people have become so suspicious, we must take to the country for it, or make use of our staff of dignity (a club). Oh! the country—the country by all means—the country for ever, where the people are so good-natured, and the chickens fat, and ready for roasting. The country is the place. When I lived out of town I was never without a fowl or a lamb for market; many a windfall; and only two or three times in the brig (prison).

"'Faith comrade, we're not badly lodged here, it's true, but we can't live upon nothing; we'll have to set to work to-morrow in earnest.— You'll take charge of the upper town market. I'll make my bargains in that of the lower town, and hang me, if to-morrow at dinner-time, we have not something to make a stew of.

"'I've another plan. What's to prevent us visiting the Island of Orleans; there's a harvest to be gathered there; plenty of sheep, and the easiest thing in the world to catch them. Just throw them on their backs—so—a wisp of hay in their mouth, and the lamb's your own.'

"'That would not be a bad idea at all, but then we require a boat of some kind.'

"'Well, we'll think of it; meantime let's have a whet, for we certainly deserve one.'"

"So saying, the two men entered abruptly the apartment in which I was. I recognized them immediately as two labourers often employed in our lumber yard; their names were Mathieu and Charboneau. Mrs. A—— had let them a little room about eight feet square, the entrance to which was through a window. Seeing me, they accosted me familiarly.

"'Boss,' said one of the two, 'you'll do to get us out of our difficulty; we've a nest to rob, and want a boat. You'll lend us yours for a night, to get a few fat sheep from the Island of Orleans.'

"I refused them promptly. 'I'll see you to the ——,' said I, 'before I'll lend my boat to go stealing with.'

"'Stealing! who said anything about stealing? But it's all right, we'll hear what Cambray will have to say to it.'

"At this moment in walked Cambray himself, who only replied to their request by a laugh of scorn. 'Bah! sheep stealers; are you fools? But I'll tell you what, Mathieu, if you know where to find a well-lined purse in any of these country parishes, that would be worth seeing to, and I wouldn't mind taking a share of the risks.'

"'Yes, deuce take it, I do know where to look for one. There's an old bachelor living near St Laurent Church; he must have some three hundred pounds concealed somewhere on the premises.'

"Accordingly the whole four of us started for the Island—Cambray, Mathieu, Charboneau, and myself, and in a short time found ourselves at the residence of the aforesaid old bachelor; it was situated in the very centre of the village, at but a short distance from the church.

"The night we had chosen was one of the most beautiful; the great harvest moon sailed majestically above, bathing the surrounding landscape in a flood of soft light, as brilliant, almost, as if it had been day.

"Without losing a moment, Mathieu stepped up to the window and took out a pane of glass. 'Take care,' said Cambray, 'remember there must be no violence unless we are absolutely driven to it.'

"The pane fell and broke in pieces. I trembled with fear; it was the first time I had witnessed a proceeding of that nature, and I took to my heels and ran like a traitor. When at about the distance of an acre, I turned my head, and seeing my companions close upon my heels, I redoubled my efforts to escape, followed by them as hard as they could go.

"'What's the matter? what frightened you?' said one; 'what did you see?' said another. 'Stop, stop.' But I pushed on in an agony of fear.

"At last, having ran upwards of a mile, I could go no further; and Cambray coming up again, roared out, 'What the d—— did you see, Waterworth? Tell us what you saw.'

"'Nothing,' said I overcome with horror, 'but—but—'

"'What! you saw nothing, and you ran in that way. What a confounded coward you must be.' But my strength was so spent, that I could hardly breathe.

"Shortly after, the day began to dawn, and it

became useless to re-attempt our expedition that night. Mathieu, however, insisted upon giving us a specimen of his skill in sheep stealing; after which we returned to the city, and wound up our proceedings by an excellent repast on roast lamb, which we had at Mrs. A——'s.

"Some days after our abortive expedition to the Island of Orleans, we planned a visit to the country house of a Mrs. Atkinson; the premises were well known both to Cambray and myself, for we had had, frequently, business transactions at the place.

"This project was also ratified at Mrs. A——'s, and the parties who had assisted us in our former scheme, were also our accomplices in this.

"Mathieu, by way of precaution, entered into a private understanding with some of his fellow-labourers, to the effect, that should the booty, by any chance, slip through our hands, they would take measures to secure it. Nevertheless, we were not destined to succeed this time either, for, whether through remorse or fear, no sooner was the first ice broken, than I again took flight. So that our second enterprise met with the same fate as our first.

"A few days afterwards, November 3, 1834, two old scoundrels, J. Stewart, and J. H——l, came one evening to the residence of Cambray, and proposed that he should accompany them in the robbery of Mr. Atkinson's, observing at the same time that it was dangerous to let the fruit ripen any longer, as all their confréres were using every effort to obtain it. I was asleep at the time, but they awoke me, and I solemnly promised that this time I would not desert my post, and before leaving, we each of us pledged ourselves to secresy, by repeating the following sentence:

"'In the Devil's name, kill me if I blab.'

"We went by boats as far as the East India wharf, where we parted with Stewart and H——l; we then rowed to the market place, where they again met us, in order to inform us that they had succeeded in opening the yard door, unseen.— We then all proceeded to the place. A crossbar is lifted without noise. Cambray and H——l were soon inside, while Stewart and I kept watch without. Our comrades found the safe, but tried in vain to remove it; at last Cambray, irritated to excess, and cursing his soul, seized hold of it, and by a violent effort, he raised it against his person, and with a firm step, placed it on the window, where we, coming to his aid, slid it carefully into the yard by means of a plank. How Cambray managed to lift so great a weight I cannot tell; I am sure it could not have been less than eight cwt., for it was only by great labour that we managed to get it to the boat. But to proceed. Off we went with our prize, and shortly after we came to anchor on a sand bank in the river St. Charles; this bank is immediately opposite the St. Paul's market, and is always dry at low tide. Waiting until the ford was passable, Cambray hastened to fetch an axe, with which we broke open the chest, and tying up the contents in two handkerchiefs, we made our way back to his house. There, in a private chamber, did we take an inventory of our spoils; the lion's share, as usual, falling to Cambray; for while he kept me employed in burning the

papers and books of the establishment, he managed to pocket the money before the very eyes of the others, whom he put off with a few dollars. Next day he gave me seven pounds. I have since learned that the box contained one hundred and fifty pounds; so that this night's work was worth five hundred dollars to Cambray.

"Stewart was arrested on suspicion for this robbery, and in consequence, passed two months in prison as a vagabond.

"The excitement over, I left for Broughton, where I remained until the end of January, 1835, when Cambray came to urge me to return to Quebec; and to avoid giving rise to any suspicions, he had me summoned to appear as a witness in a case then pending between him and a tavern keeper named D——l—t. This was, of course, a mere pretext for I knew nothing whatever about the matter. However, I returned with him, and we shall now see by what new exploits we distinguished ourselves.

CHAPTER V.

Expedition to Carouge—Mrs. O.—A practical joke—Burglary at Paradis', Charlesbourg.

"Arrived at Quebec, and Cambray and I recommenced our visits to Mrs. A.'s, where we found Mathieu and G—g—n still residing, with whom we renewed our intimacy, and plotted further depredations. Among other plans, it was proposed that we should visit an old man named Paradis, who lived at Caprouge, so we were told, and who, it was said, possessed a large amount of money. Cambray and myself undertook to make all the necessary enquiries, and be ready by the next day; this we did, but with scarcely any success. On coming to the place, we found that Paradis had left some time before, and that he then lived at Charlesbourg. An old woman, Mrs. O—, occupied the house with her daughter, where they kept a sort of tavern. As soon as we got back to the city, we hastened to our rendezvous, and informed our associates of the particulars.

"'A propos,' said Mathieu, 'the old woman you speak of ought to have laid up a little money; she and her daughter have been some time in business. What do you say to try that casket to-night?'

"'What would be the use of it?' said I. 'I know the poor woman well, and am satisfied there is not a half-penny to be found in the house unless, indeed, the little we may have left.'

"'Never mind, we can try.'

"And try we did. We burst open the door with iron levers, and in we went, without further ceremony.

"The poor women, frightened almost out of their lives, escaped through a window at the back. We pursued, and obliged them to return, though sorely against their will; then, opening the cellar door, we pushed them in, where Cambray and Mathieu followed.

"'The cellar is the most valuable room in the house,' said Gagnon; 'we could never have done without it.'

"All this took place in the dark, a most necessary precaution with us, considering we never made use of masks.

" Our birds caged, we struck a light, and whilst our companions were indulging in their interesting *tête-a-tête*, we saw no reason why we should not enjoy ourselves too; accordingly, we placed a table over the cellar trap, and having furnished it with edibles and drinkables, down we sat, and enjoyed ourselves heartily. Need I say our friends soon joined us, and we had a roaring time of it.

" Supper over, we loaded the trap-door with everything we could lay our hands on—stove, boxes, pots, stewpans—everything. This completed, we set to work to pillage the house, and having appropriated the best articles of clothing we could find, together with a few pieces of silver, we exhorted our fair prisoners to bear patiently with their lot, and bade them farewell.

" The following day was dedicated to a new excursion.

" Cambray and I went to hunt up old Paradis, whom we found with little difficulty; and Cambray, by way of accounting for his presence, asked him the way to Lake Beauport.

" But we did not, however, succeed in informing ourselves sufficiently with respect to the general arrangements of the premises, and Gagnon and I returned the next day to complete our survey. This time, Gagnon pretended he wanted to find *Craig's mill*, showing at the same time the address, which had been written on a piece of paper; for my part, I kept out of the way, fearing he might recognize my figure. Having returned to Cambray's, and acquainted him with our observations, that evening we all started on our expedition. This happened, I believe, on the 3rd February, 1835.

" Crowbars in hand, we threw ourselves all together on the door, which gave way instantaneously to the shock, and in a moment we were in the first room. Judge of our surprise on entering, to find an old grey-headed man on his knees, trembling fearfully, his hands raised to Heaven, to whom he was crying, ' mercy, mercy—a thousand times mercy.'

" This man was an old beggar, who had taken up his lodgings there for the night. His fears and his prayers set us all in a roar of laughter. One of us seized the fellow, another rushed at old Paradis, who was in bed at the time, dragged him out by the neck, and a third opening the cellar trap, they were both hurled in to keep each other company.

" I sought to enter a little sleeping apartment, at the door of which I found myself.

" ' Don't go in there,' said Cambray ; ' let us do the thing orderly, and divide fairly and brotherly.'

" ' Leave me alone,' said I, ' there's a pretty girl inside—the niece of the old man.'

" ' Stay with us—stay with us, I tell you, or you're a dead man.'

" I was obliged to obey. On breaking open a box, we found a great quantity of gold coin. This Cambray put in his pocket.

" Having made the stove red hot, we determined upon taking Paradis out of the cellar, and seating him upon it. This was to induce a speedy confession on his part with regard to his places of concealment.

" It was an operation we had frequently to resort to in the cases of the unruly—the naughty—children who did not submit gracefully to our persuasiveness ; but we were startled by the discovery that some one had escaped by the window of the room which I had intended entering ; the girl, doubtless.

" This gave us so much alarm that we made our escape as hastily as possible. When we were at some distance, Gagnon shewed us a pistol he had wrenched from Paradis.

" On the road home, Cambray, coming close to me, said softly, almost in a whisper, ' Let us try and humbug Gagnon and Mathieu ; here, hide this,' and he threw me eighteen doubloons and fifteen dollars. The remainder he slipped adroitly into the linings of his trousers and into his boots.

" Arrived at his residence, he drew forth a few dollars ; he gave sixteen to Gagnon and Mathieu as their share. For my part, I received forty-eight, and he retained the balance, which must have been upwards of six hundred dollars, seeing that we had laid Paradis under a contribution of one hundred and seventy pounds.

" Matters continued pretty much in this way ; when we were in humour, we went on with our work. On one occasion we broke into the office of a Mr. Parke, a merchant in the Lower Town, and there we found little silver and a telescope, which Cambray appropriated, ' to gratify a whim,' he said.

" Up to this time we lived in the greatest hardihood. We were suspected by nobody, and we had the pleasure each day of listening to the details of our brigandage, and of moralizing thereon, Cambray and I mixing with the most respectable society. When suspicion became aroused, and we were incarcerated, the telescope, of which I have spoken, was found and identified. Nevertheless Cambray escaped punishment in this instance.

" Emboldened by these successes, we did not stop, but pushed our robberies even into the Chapel of the Congregation, the details of which audacious attempt may be found in the trial of Gagnon."

CHAPTER VI.

Sacrilegious Robbery of the Chapel of "La Congregation"—Trial of Gagnon—Verdict.

So far we have taken our narrative from the lips of the witness. We will now, for the moment, adopt another form, as being suited to our purpose, and obtain our details from the trial itself, namely, the sacrilegious robbery of the R. C. Chapel of the Congregation.

During the night of the 9th and 10th February, 1835, the R. C. Chapel of the Congregation of Quebec, was forcibly entered, and value stolen therefrom to the amount of £92 10s., namely : a silver lamp, £20 ; a crucifix, £10 ; a statue of the Virgin, £50 ; four sconces, £10 ; and two candlesticks, £2 10s.

On the 29th March, 1837, Pierre Gagnon was arraigned before the Criminal Court, charged with having been an accomplice in the robbery of the Congregational Chapel, together with Charles Cambray and George Waterworth. The accused was a man young in years, but

aged in crime ; nor was this his first appearance
at the criminal bar. Repulsive in appearance,
and possessed of a harsh and disagreeable voice,
it was evident his career had been nursed within
the walls of a prison, and was likely to be ex-
piated only on the gallows.

Messrs. Cazault, chaplain ; Joseph Dubois,
sexton ; Joseph Peticlerc, syndic ; and Etienne
Metivier, watchman, were held as witnesses to
testify, both to the robbery and the value of the
effects stolen ; and in addition to these, was
George Waterworth, an accomplice in the crime,
who had turned king's evidence, in the hope of
pardon.

In the month of February, 1835, the witness,
Waterworth, resided with Cambray.

At about eight o'clock on the evening of the
robbery, they went to Mrs. Anderson's, where
they found Mathieu and Gagnon, who still lived
in the same place. Having drunk together,
Cambray entered into conversation with Gagnon and Mâthieu, but in a very low tone of
voice ; taking an opportunity, when Mrs. Anderson was absent for a moment, the two last named
slipped out and returned shortly afterwards with
a crowbar. They then left the premises, and
walked through St. Louis Gate towards the
Esplanade ; it was not, however, until they
arrived at the chapel that they fully resolved
upon entering it. But there were difficulties in
the way—people were seen to remain near it for
some time—so, to avoid suspicion, the robbers
continued their walk towards St. John's Gate,
and then returned to the spot in question by a
different route. The people had gone. Mathieu
and Gagnon then approached the door of the
building, and worked some time to effect an
entrance. As soon as they had succeeded in
forcing it open, one of them returned to where
Cambray was, and said to him : "Now that the
door is open, you may walk in." The witness
further said that he perceived they had broken
half of a window above the door ; the aperture
was sufficiently large to admit the body of a
man, and he believed that it must have been by
this means that one of them had entered, and
thus been enabled to open the door from the
inside. But to proceed : Mathieu and the two
others glided into the chapel, leaving Waterworth to keep watch without, and give alarm in
case of discovery, or, in the event of its being
occasioned by one person only, to silence him
with a blow from a club he carried.

The three remained inside about a quarter of
an hour, during which time they lit a candle,
with phosphoric matches purchased by Cambray
from Sims, an apothecary in the Upper Town.
They then wrapped the stolen articles in mantles
and in the woman's attire with which Gagnon
and Mathieu had been disguised on this occasion. This over, they returned to Mrs. Anderson's ; but fearing that their movements might
attract observation, they transported their booty
to Cambray's. Entering by a yard at the back,
they introduced themselves into a hay-loft,
where they again struck a light and examined
the result of their expedition. Here it was that
the witness first set eyes upon the effects, which
he observed consisted of a silver image of the
Virgin, a lamp, and several candlesticks ; he

also recollected that it was a matter of debate
whether one of the candlesticks was of pure
silver. He remembered breaking it with an
axe to ascertain the truth ; they found it to be
only plated. They then descended into the
stable, and having raised one of the planks, they
concealed everything beneath it.

A few days after this affair, Mathieu and
Gagnon returned to demand their share of the
spoils. As Cambray was absent at the time—
he had gone out with his wife—the witness gave
them each a dollar or two, and told them to arrange with Cambray for the rest. Later on,
Waterworth and Cambray made up their minds
to take the silver to Broughton, where, as we
have stated, the relatives of the former then
lived. Accordingly, they procured two barrels,
one of which they filled with liquor, and into
the other they put the ornaments of the Congregational Chapel. Waterworth then started for
Broughton ; he was driven there in a cariole by a
carter ; and besides the barrels, he brought with
him several other articles. He arrived there on
the second day from the time of his departure,
having slept a night at a tavern kept by one
Morin, near St. Mary's.

Having stowed the barrels within doors, and
given special instructions to his sister with regard
to them, he drew from one a jar full of liquor,
which he carried to the house of a man named
Stevens, who lived at the further end of the
township. In this visit he was accompanied by
his sister, his brother-in-law, a man of the name
of Knox, and the carter. The witness remained
the whole night here ; but when Knox was on
the point of leaving, he desired him to conceal
the larger barrel in the snow. This was done.

Cambray made his appearance a few days
after this ; and he and Waterworth having
satisfied themselves as to the safety of the
barrel, they both returned to Quebec. Scarcely
had they arrived, however, than they learned that
Carrier, the constable, had left for Broughton. This happened on Ash Wednesday. Fearful of discovery, and determined at all risks
to ward off the impending blow, the robbers
started after him on the following day, and
travelled nearly fifty miles between five o'clock
in the afternoon and one the following morning.
On the road they met Carrier returning, and,
doubtful as to the issue of his journey, they
accosted him, asking him where he had been.
He answered that he had been to Broughton on
several business matters. They continued ques-
tioning him ; but, receiving very evasive answers,
Waterworth, to make sure that he had discovered
nothing, pretended to be drunk, and insisted
upon searching the constable's cariole, under
the pretence of looking for liquor ; but finding
nothing, they continued their journey.

Arrived at Broughton, the witness made
special enquiries respecting the object of Carrier's visit. His father, who appeared deeply
affected by the thought that his house, which
had hitherto enjoyed an unexceptional character,
should have been made an object of search by
the police, told him that the constable had been
there, but had found nothing. This ascer-
tained, Cambray decided upon leaving immediately for the city, from which he re-

turned in the commencement of the following April, bringing with him two crucibles, a bushel of coal, and a pair of bellows. The following night, Cambray, Norris, Knox, and the witness, retired to the adjoining woods, where they made a fire in the sugar cabin, and endeavoured to melt their silver; but being unable to attain this, they broke it into pieces with a hammer, and having rolled it up in a cloth, Cambray and Waterworth brought it back to Quebec.

On Easter eve, the two associates carried their silver to the quarries at Caprouge, where they broke into a house used by the workmen, who were then absent. They found the key of the blacksmith's forge, and having kindled the fire, they placed their silver once more in the crucibles they had procured, and again submitted them to the action of the flames, beating and flattening the pieces at times with the heavy mallets they found in the place, in order to quicken the process as much as possible.

Thus they passed Easter Sunday, undisturbed by a single accident, the fire being so ardent as to cause one of the crucibles to crack. As the image of the child, held in the arms of the virgin, was found to resist alike flame and physical force, Cambray, who held it in his hand, turned to Waterworth, and said:

"Just look at this unlucky imp. He will give us as much trouble as Shadrach, Meshach, and Abednego."

Nevertheless, towards evening, they had reduced all into ingots, which Cambray carried home with him, and which remained in his possession.

The prisoner here cross-questioned the witness as follows:

Prisoner—"Do you believe that you have a soul?"
Witness—"Yes; I believe that I have a soul to save."
Prisoner—"Have you never borne false witness?"
Witness—"No, never."
Prisoner—"What! Did you not swear falsely when you said that Cambray was not present at the murder of Sivrac?"
The Court exempted the witness from answering this question.

Several witnesses were then heard to corroborate the evidence given by the accomplice, as follows:

Mrs. Anderson, to prove the interview held by the accused at her house; Cecilia Connor George Hall, and Eliza Lapointe, to confirm the transactions which had taken place at Broughton; and René Labbé, blacksmith, to give evidence in connection with the use of his forge on Easter Sunday.

The accused then read the following appeal to the jury, from a paper which he held in his hand.

"Gentlemen of the Jury.—It is with sincere sorrow that I behold myself forced to address you on an occasion like the present, one which will deprive me of my life, if you consider me guilty of the crime whereof I stand accused. My situation is the more pitiable, as I occupy the position of another, whose substitute I am.

"Waterworth, the king's evidence in this case, the only witness who implicates me in the robbery of the Congregational Chapel, has placed me in the position of one of his own relations, Norris, the husband of his sister. To save him, he destroys me; to screen a relative, he delivers an innocent man over to the sword of justice. I pray of you to reflect upon this, and also upon the character of him who deposes against me. It is the man, who, only a year ago, perjured himself before this very Court, when he said that Cambray was not the author of Sivrac's murder, committed at Lotbinière, and in which he himself was complicated. He swore in the face of God and man, that he had seen him purchase the same silver spoons he, the witness, had assisted him to steal. Had I the means, I could prove this assertion on the oath of no less than eight persons; but, enclosed within the prison for eighteen months, without money, and without protection, what was it possible for me to effect? The subpœnas which I had procured a few days before this term, were taken from me by my fellow prisoners.

"The man who denounces me is he who avowed himself an accomplice in the robbery committed at Mrs. Montgomery's—a being without shame—one who entered even a church, and seized upon the sacred property, to the insult of divinity; and he it was who conducted the various robberies in the Lower Town, and broke open and pillaged the counting-houses. Yes, it is upon this man's conscience, unsupported by other evidence, that I am now accounted his accomplice, whereas it is upon Norris, whom it is his interest to conceal, that the odium ought to attach itself. Such is the man whose testimony you have to consider.

"Remember, that, even in this Court, there have been instances in which the innocent have suffered for the guilty. In the case of a robbery committed against a Mr. Masse, of Point Levi, the Crown witness accused four persons entirely free from blame, when suddenly another appeared, whose evidence led to the conviction of the real offenders. The man who thus perjured himself was Ross, who was afterwards executed, and whose case created so deep a sensation in this city. Remember, too, there are in Quebec a great number of thieves who have the wit to place their deeds of darkness to the account of old delinquents; men who, having already appeared at the criminal bar, are more likely to be thought guilty. I admit that it is my misfortune to bear an infamous character, and to my disgrace I have already appeared before this tribunal; but if I have been guilty, I have suffered severely for my crime.

"If my reputation is bad, the more open is it to suspicion. Pay, then, no attention to the career of my past life—deign only to consider the state of my present position.

"On the evening of the 10th April, on which the crime was committed, I passed the whole night at Mrs. Anderson's, as also a girl who could give her evidence to this effect, but that she is now in the State of Maine. Another girl called Doren could, if alive, have confessed this; but Waterworth, quarrelling with her, beat her so violently, that on the following day she was found dead on St. Louis street. I can, however, produce a woman named Catherine Rocque, who slept at Mrs. Anderson's on the same night.

"Having now submitted my defence, I desire not that you sacrifice conscience for my sake. All I ask is that you will render me justice. May God assist you in your verdict."

The prisoner had but one witness, the girl, Catherine Rocque, whom we have already mentioned, and who happened at that time to be in prison. She was, however, brought before the prisoner with the following result :

Prisoner—" I ask you, Miss Rocque, do you know me ?"

Witness—" Yes."

Prisoner—" Were you not at Mrs. Anderson's on the 9th April, two years ago ?"

Witness—" Yes."

Prisoner—" Did not I sleep there that night ?"

Witness—" Yes ; I believe you did. That was two years ago, was it not ?"

Prisoner—" Did not I remain there the whole night ? Was not I tipsy ?"

Witness—" I do not know whether you remained all night, for I was a little mellow myself. I went to bed at six in the morning, and did not get up till the following day."

Prisoner—" Enough ; I have nothing further to ask."

In the course of the trial, Mr. O. Stewart, counsel for Cambray, took exception to one of the heads of the accusation, namely : that of sacrilege—raising the question whether the Congregational Chapel ought to rank with churches, the robbery of which the law designates sacrilege, and the Court took this question *en délibéré.*

The Honorable Judge Bowen then addressed the jury. He recapitulated the evidence furnished by the trial; he dwelt at some length on the various points necessary to be taken into consideration before rendering a verdict, the principal one being doubtless the caution with which they ought to receive the testimony of the Crown witnesses, observing that it ought to be accepted or rejected only so far as it agreed with the statements of other witnesses. "The jurors," he added, " had before them a question of a very delicate nature—one that touched directly on the conscience of each individual, the dictates of which would doubtless tell them whether he had spoken the truth, or whether he had disguised it.

The jury then retired, and shortly after returned their verdict, namely : " That Pierre Gagnon was guilty of sacrilege, or grand larceny, to the value of £20."

Such was the decision of the Court on the objection taken by Mr. Stewart.

CHAPTER VII.

Suspicions—Conspiracy against Waterworth—Another Expedition to the Island of Orleans.

Waterworth here resumes the thread of his narrative :

The sacrilegious robbery of the Congregational Chapel gave us so much trouble, and was the cause of so much research on the part of the police, who all but discovered our tracks, that for some time afterwards we were obliged to remain inactive. We began at that time to feel a little distrustful of our security, and it was the following incident that gave birth to our suspicions :

One hundred pounds having been offered by the Governor for the discovery of the guilty, a sum sufficiently great to tempt the cupidity of most people, a woman being at Mrs. Anderson's on the evening of the robbery, and having observed us leaving the place, imagined that possibly we might be connected with the affair. Accordingly she found Carrier, the constable, and proposed to communicate her suspicions to him, on the condition that if they led to the conviction of the offenders, she was to obtain half the sum advertised.

Carrier, on his part, mentioned the circumstance to certain friends of ours, from whom it came to our ears, and it was upon me that the accusers had fastened as their victim. For this reason were my journeys to Broughton undertaken. As for Cambray, his name as yet remained untouched.

Great was the discomfiture of these greedy beings, when they found that their efforts had terminated in naught; but Carrier may thank heaven that he had nothing in his cariole at the time we met him ; for had it been otherwise, we would most certainly have saved him his journey home. Our determination to murder him was fixed, and every step towards its accomplishment had been taken with great precaution.

I believe, however, that on these occasions we permitted a spirit of indulgence, of humanity, to triumph over common sense ; for to this systematic lenity I cannot but attribute much that led to our discovery. True, it was not immediate in its effects ; nevertheless it brought on further and better founded accusations. In fact, I am of opinion that it was the movements of Carrier that furnished Cecelia Connor with the suspicions that we had the church silver in our possession, suspicions which gradually strengthened, until, in the summer of 1835, they were laid before the Court as facts, on which were based our arrest ; for it must not be forgotten that this woman was entirely ignorant of the contents of the larger barrel, nor could she have overheard any conversation concerning it. Her discovery, therefore, must have sprung entirely from her imagination ; but this is only conjecture, for the incident has ever been a mystery to us, something we have never been able to comprehend.

"Stop a moment ! Possibly you may not have heard that she followed you into the wood—that she saw the image of the Virgin in the hands of Cambray—that from Knox she took a small silver sceptre, that ——"

" Is it possible, is it possible? *she* watched us, spied out our retreat, discovered us in the act. Ah ! had we only known, how easy it would have been to have prevented all this trouble. I could never have imagined that imbecile old creature, such as she is, could have dared to watch us after that manner. Had I thought it possible, I would have strangled her without any remorse whatsoever. Personal safety is the first law of nature. Did she then follow us ? Alone ? into the woods? Ah, that I could meet her once more."

In giving way to this burst of passion, the witness betrayed the secret working of his heart; he showed himself in the fulness of his wickedness, the strength of his ferocious nature completely overpowered every other consideration, and usurped at once the mild sentiments of contrition and regret to which he had hitherto expressed himself resigned. He rose in his seat, his fists clenched, and his lips quivering with emotion—he was indeed the picture of a bloodthirsty villain. Shortly after he seemed gradually to suppress all external symptoms of agitation; he remained quite silent for a considerable space of time, and finally relapsed into that marble-like coldness which had hitherto characterised his address. He continued :

After the chapel silver had been reduced to ingots, and deposited in a place of safety, I went home to Broughton, from which I returned about the middle of May.

On my arrival, we set about a new expedition. This was our first work of the kind since the sacrilege ; it took place on the Island of Orleans. There were four of us concerned in the affair—Cambray, Mathieu, Knox, and myself ; but Knox knew nothing of our conspiracy, he had only come to take charge of the boat. We proceeded to the parish of St. Laurent, where we broke open the house of an old bachelor. We found him alone, and seized him by the throat, in bed. He tried to resist, so that we were obliged to treat him to a few strokes of a stick. Our expedition ended in nothing, for we found no money ; nor can I believe he possessed any, after the proofs to which he submitted. For want of something better, we carried off his stock of provisions, and some of his best wearing apparel. I admit it was a piece of cruelty to trouble a poor old man for so little profit.

The following was much more satisfactory, and gave us much less trouble. It was the robbery committed at Mrs. Montgomery's, the interesting details of which are given in the trial of Cambray and Mathieu.

CHAPTER VIII.

Carouge Wood—The Robbers' Retreat—Mathieu—
Stewart and Lemire—A Conspiracy.

About three o'clock in the afternoon of the 22nd May, 1835, two men passed through St. Lewis Suburbs, and directed their steps towards the plains of Abraham.

"For that business," said Waterworth in a low tone to his companion Cambray, "we will require at least seven or eight determined fellows. Remember, it is in the very centre of the town."

"Bah, seven or eight men to strangle a few women, and pillage a house. You are nothing but a coward, and know nothing about it ; the more accomplices we have, *the smaller will be our profits;* besides that, it does not do to bring too many into affairs of that kind—some traitor."

"Oh, as to that you are right enough ; it does

not do to trust our secrets to everybody. In an unlucky moment, we might be intimidated, and through weakness or remorse, or even treason, one might be obliged to swallow his own dose, in order to save himself. This is doubtless true."

"A thousand devils ; if ever accomplice plays me that trick, if ever I even *suspect* that any one dared to think of such a thing, he would not remain a sound man much longer. I'd soon make him forget the taste of his victuals."

"For that reason we ought to select men of energy and trust," said Waterworth, a little embarrassed, "men capable of even sacrificing themselves, if necessary, rather than utter a dangerous word. If Dumas was not in prison now, he would answer capitally ; he's a crafty rogue."

"Dumas, he never attempts anything on a large scale ; he is too fearful of a dance in the air. I have already told you Mathieu is one I am looking for ; he's the very man, desperate as a devil, fearing neither heaven nor earth—cunning, cool, discreet, full of energy, and, above all, able to force a lock better than any man living. He is, moreover, one of whom we need have no suspicion—a miserable old valet, who is unconscious of his own abilities, and is incapable of turning them to account. A few dollars to drink, and be merry, is all he will ask; his aim will be no higher than a night's debauchery. In addition to him, we might find a couple of second rate thieves, whom we could pay so much for the night."

"Certes, Mathieu ; let it be so, then, since he is the best, and we will find two others as assistants only."

"Still we will be very few," said Waterworth ; and here the two companions jumped over a fence, and discovered at a short distance a group of men and woman. It was the band they were in search of.

The plains of Abraham, and the neighbouring woods, particularly that of Carouge, are the *rendezvous* of a certain industrial class, who find it more convenient to live upon the goods of their neighbours than to earn any for themselves. These men are the outcasts of society, branded with infamy, united by crime, and in league against the law ; having no other resource, their lives are spent in plotting against justice, surrounded by perpetual misery and fear. They know neither peace nor security, nor do they even enjoy the regular pittance of the poor. At one time they are glutted with their prey; at another they are almost dying with hunger. On the open hills they hold their gatherings, and spend their nights the victims of infamy and terror.

They know not the repose of honesty, fearful visions haunt them day and night ; they have not even the consolation of friendship—those they meet in this place are destitute of either feeling or sympathy—all sentiments of nature are dead within them—interest, purely personal interest, is the strongest passion they know, and baseness, calumny and treason is their current change. When in the spring of the year the prisons are emptied, when navigation throws her hordes of divers people upon our shores, this infected body spreads over our fields, and mutineers, adventurers, bullies and debauched characters add daily to its numbers.

Should you trust yourself within the precincts mentioned, you do so at a considerable risk, for if your appearance indicates *contribution*, some four of these rascals seize you by the throat, levy their toll, and fly, leaving you half dead upon the spot.

In the adjoining woods they have their hiding places, their *rendezvous*, and their caves, and in the neighbourhood their taverns and their courts.

When they have succeeded in making a good haul, a feast is sure to follow; the kettle is suspended to the branch of some tree, the fowl is cooked in open air, and eaten on the grass; the moon and stars preside over amourous meetings, disgusting orgies, iniquitous conspiracies, and short and restless repose.

Astonishing as it may seem, these hardened and unnatural beings are the slaves of women even more infamous than themselves; for them they commit their thefts, for them they stake their very existence, and for them they waste in prodigality all they have acquired at the peril of their lives. Even here, amid the corrupt and the wicked, love reigns triumphant, asserting its power over the human heart, even when that heart is dead to all other feelings of humanity. Before its omnipotence, every other passion bows, and in its grasp all are helpless.

But it would be too fearful to reveal the scenes of bloodshed to which it has given rise in the woods of Carouge—to relate the jealousies, the retaliations, and the murders it has occasioned in this place; but which are now buried in oblivion, through the apathy and indifference of the beholders.

" Ah, the idle scamps," said Cambray, as they neared the group, who had already noticed their arrival. " Look at them running; look, they take us for constables. Ha, ha, ha—those gentlemen are never quite sure of being innocent."

Notwithstanding the state of excitement into which the ragged assemblage was thrown, four or five of the vagabonds refused to budge, for they had recognised their visitors, and heartily enjoyed the confusion their presence had occasioned.

Cambray now left his companion, and, advancing to them, placed his hand familiarly on the shoulder of one of them—a man of about forty years of age, of middling stature, slightly made, and marked with small-pox. He had a pale complexion, sparklingly black and vivacious eyes, a narrow and lowering forehead, thick hair, and uneven and hoarse voice, large whiskers coming up almost to his eyes, thin ears, an extremely small mouth, and the entire expression of his features sharp and angular. Altogether, his physiognomy was stamped with the ferocity of a brute rather than the character of a man.

" Mathieu (for it was he), Mathieu," said Cambray, " I've a secret for you."

" What ?" replied the man springing up from where he was, and striking his sides. " What ? A nest to rob ? Speak—I'm your man."

" Well, comrade, you remember I have frequently spoken to you of Mrs. Montgomery, but as yet we have done nothing in the matter; that there is money there, you know. What do you say to giving us your help ? We have almost forgotten our trade, so long is it since we have worked at it; but remember, perseverance and perfect coolness are indispensable. Be secret and courageous, my boy, and the chicken is ours."

" Courage ! the devil knows well enough I'm not the man to be frightened; and as to secresy, I should think twenty years service have taught me that. I will be ready this evening, if you wish; the night will be dark, there will be no moon, and killing may be done without fear."

" Let it be so," said Cambray, " give me your hand for this evening; but we shall want assistance. Three will never be able to manage it, and that great calf there (pointing to Waterworth) is little better than a drowned hen. Perhaps you are acquainted with some worthy children, able scamps, who might be useful ?"

" Scamps ! plenty of them; but as to their being able, that's another question. However, there are some clever numsculls. Stewart, for instance, is a wily fox, and well-suited for our purpose. Then there's Lemire, a young hand, it is true, but with plenty of pluck, soul enough for a beef-eater ; he would be worth something."

" But you forget Gagnon," said Waterworth, coming up; " he was an old servant of the lady's, and could give us a good deal of advice."

" His advice," said Cambray. " Pooh ! I have sounded him long ago. Never fear, I know his secret, and that's all we want; he would ask too much for his services."

" It will teach him in future not to tell where his nests may be found," said Mathieu, " by my faith, but it will be a rare trick to cook the pear without his knowledge—he who has reckoned upon it for such a length of time. Hallo! Stewart—Lemire—come here, my boys."

At this call two men left the group of thieves, who were lying at a short distance, jealous of being excluded from the secret of the conspiracy which was apparently on foot, and came forward to join their three friends. One of them was a man of about thirty-six years of age, small in stature, but well made, and with rather a passable countenance, considerably at variance with his character, although somewhat severe in expression. This man was an old delinquent, named Stewart, not so much that he was a great criminal as a vicious and corrupt being. The other was much more characteristic and revolting in physiognomy; his copper-coloured skin, like that of an Indian—his demon-like eyes, his pointed and ill-formed head, his gait, his sharp and cunning visage, his figure, his countenance—all bespoke him of dark and dogged disposition, well fitted for the paths of vice. This man could not have been more than twenty years of age ; his name was Lemire. He had already appeared on several different occasions at the bar of justice, accused of crimes committed with a fearful degree of audacity, nor had he even escaped the last and solemn sentence of death.

Some years ago, it will be remembered, that an Irishman, crossing the Plains with his dearer half, whom he had only espoused that morning, and was now about to introduce to his future habitation and his home, was attacked in open day by a band of four robbers. Happily, the bridegroom was a man of considerable physical strength, had a brave heart, and plenty of nerve. Disarming one of his adversaries, he struck them to the ground, and succeeded in making three of them prisoners. Lemire was one of them; he it was who commenced the attack.

"Come along, my game cocks," said Mathieu; "come along, we want you here. What do you say to distinguishing yourselves this evening at——"

"Hush, hush," interposed Cambray, putting his hand over Mathieu's mouth; "secrecy or death—secrecy or *death*—Mathieu, remember *that*. Let all of you come and see me this evening, and you'll know the rest. Mathieu, you'll bring them; hide yourselves under the window, and we'll meet you a little after dusk. Good bye."

So saying, he started off with his companion, and the brigands returned to their party.

CHAPTER IX.

The Young Wife: her fears—The Rendezvous—Burglary at Mrs. Montgomery's.

At about half-past nine o'clock that evening, three persons were assembled in a small room. Waterworth sat silently in one corner of the apartment, his head resting on his hands; Cambray was at a table, drawing with a pencil the divisions of a spacious dwelling; and opposite him sat a young woman of singularly mild and agreeable countenance, delicately made, and apparently in very feeble health. An expression of deep melancholy rested upon her face, adding considerably to the interest of her appearance; she was, moreover, in that state which calls forth our tenderest sympathy. She was evidently in great suffering, stopping occasionally with a white handkerchief the great tears that coursed over her cheeks. A single candle, the flame of which was dimmed by a long black wick, threw a faint glimmer of light over the three figures, and added, if possible, to the solemn and mysterious silence that reigned in the apartment.

"But, my dear friend," observed the young woman, breaking for the first time the monotony of this sad tranquillity, "what sort of life have you been leading for some time past. Alas! you never stay with me now—your occupations are too numerous, your business too extensive. Take care, my dear husband, that you do not involve yourself in difficulties, or get too deeply into debt. I often fear this will be the case, and it gives me much thought and anxiety. You are no longer as you used to be; you have become agitated, melancholy, and unhappy, and you scarcely take any rest or relaxation. Oh! I fear there is trouble at your heart. Ah, can it be that you will not make your wife your confidant!"

"Oh, don't bother me," was the brutal answer of her husband; "if we were to listen to you, women, you'd have us continually stuck in the

house, like wax dolls. It is not thus a man earns a livelihood. All your fears and lamentations are nothing but the imagination of women kind. Have you not everything in the world that is necessary to your comfort?"

"Yes, it is true that we have a great deal of money; indeed, I often feel astonished at your success in such trying times as these; but have you not said that you are going away again to-morrow? What is the use of this work, my dear husband?"

"Yes, woman, I've said it, and I'll do it; and before starting I'll take a few moments to sleep in the attics."

At that moment a dog, which had hitherto lain under the table, uttered a low growl, and arose with hair on end; he rushed to the door leading to the yard, and commenced barking furiously. Waterworth made an involuntary bound, and, raising his head, his eyes met the face of his associate without, who was grinning and winking in a most significant manner.

"Well, good evening, little wife," said Cambray; "try and be a little more reasonable." Then, turning to Waterworth: "I think it is time to turn in, if we wish to make an early start."

"Charles, Charles," interrupted his wife, by way of banishing her grief. "Charles, when are you going to give me the shawl you promised? it has not yet come."

"Make yourself easy; you'll get it to-morrow, for I hope to make a little money before daylight. Good bye."

Thus speaking, followed by his companion, he ascended a somewhat crooked flight of steps, and entered a low garret of about eight feet square, containing one miserable bed; here the two brigands, finding themselves alone, burst into a hearty fit of laughter.

"She's an innocent chicken," said Cambray; "we'll give her time to get fast asleep, and then we can get out of the window. I have the ladder ready fastened."

"Are you there, friends?" whispered Cambray.

"Here," replied a black and bloated looking phantom in a corner, "here we all are, as trusty as the sword of state. I've had a good sleep already and the most charming of dreams—I dreamed we had settled for the old woman, frightened the servant, and pillaged and burnt the house."

"Charming indeed," said Cambray—"but time presses—and you," addressing Lemire and Stewart, "you know that it's to Mrs. Montgomery's we're bound,—do you know the old woman?"

"To Mrs. Montgomery's," said Lemire; by my faith but that's funny; why, I had arranged with Gagnon to pay her a visit to-morrow— It's as good as a fortune to go there; will we break her head? assassinate."—"No, no—no useless severity" said Cambray, "merely tie them up so that they won't be able to see; I'll undertake the pillage, come."

"The oath, the oath," said Waterworth, "our safety lies in that."

"Ah, yes, that's strictness, said Mathieu, "but with gentlemen of our reputation it is seldom necessary."

Cambray however obliged them to take a horrible oath, by which they bound themselves, under the penalty of death, neither to back out of the undertaking, nor part with the secret. The ceremony over, they followed each other in silence through the street, and ascended to the Upper Town.

"Ah, here's the casket," said Mathieu, throwing himself forcibly against a little yard door which gave way to the blow, and through which he entered followed by the others.

"Look at Waterworth," continued he, "I was certain he would be the last to enter—he's always a coward on occasions like this."

"I would be so easily known," said Waterworth, "but let's see who will keep the secret longest."

Above their heads stood the kitchen window, open, and through it they got into the house.

By accident, in the lower kitchen they heard the barking of a small dog, and the flooring of the upper storey resounded to the footsteps of a person who had jumped suddenly out of bed. In a moment the burglars had hidden themselves in the four corners of the room, and there they remained as fixed and silent as marble statues.

In an upper apartment, a female in the decline of age, awoke suddenly, crying in a faltering voice to her servant:

"Elizabeth! Elizabeth! did you not hear a dull sort of a sound? What is the dog barking at? Listen! listen! don't you hear? Heavens if it should be robbers!"

"Yes, I hear it," replied the girl, "it's in the kitchen; perhaps it's the window shaking with the wind."

"No, something is walking about there; let us go down and see."

"No, no, in the name of God, don't be so bold," shrieked the old woman, nearly losing her senses. "Lock the door and listen. Oh! heaven help me, I'm choking."

"What is the matter, ma'am?" whispered a little boy of ten years old, who slept upon a sofa, and who had been awakened by the noise.

These were the only persons in the house.

The robbers, though somewhat alarmed, remained quiet, scarcely allowing themselves to breathe, and listening eagerly to every sound, in the hope of discovering how many people they had to contend against. Soon, however, the house relapsed once more into a deep and painful silence, broken only by the sobs of the women, the ticking of the clock, and the interrupted occasional barking of the dog, which rushed through the different apartments snapping at every obstacle in his way.

How difficult it is to paint the sensations of the mind, to produce in truthful color, the suspense, the weariness, the suffering of the lover who waits in vain the coming of his mistress; his impatient heart overflowing with affection, with despair, and with jealousy; but however intense may be his feelings at such a moment, they are nothing, positively nothing, compared with the mental torture endured by the two poor women we have spoken of. Weak and unprotected, trembling and frightened almost to insensibility; every moment brought fresh horror to their imaginations; every moment brought them

nearer the dreaded time, when their door would be forced in, and they would behold themselves in the presence of demons on a mission of destruction, perhaps of death; when the hand of the robber would be fastened upon their throats, and the pistol or the knife gleam savagely in the hands of a merciless and powerful foe. The night wind whistling through the crevice of a window; the cracking of a board; the buzzing of an insect, were to them noises pregnant with their coming fate, noises that chilled the very blood in their hearts, and petrified their frames with fear. To await danger in a state such as this, is to suffer a thousand deaths; it is to live beneath the millstone, and feel the crushing of your bones; to be exposed to the points of a thousand needles, and feel them entering your flesh, and tearing you to pieces; or to be present at a festival of spectres and feel their ghastly faces near your own; to behold them writhing in hideousness, and to be forced to listen to the frightful imprecations they pour into your ear. It is to endure all these at once till the mind borders on insanity, the brain reels, and the body succumbs before the dread phantom of despair. Such was the trial these unfortunate creatures had to endure for nearly an hour, between their first alarm and their second."

"Elizabeth, I hope they are gone," said the old woman, faintly, coming gradually to her senses. "I will lie down again, but I do not think I shall be able to sleep; let us wait for a moment however."

During this interval, the robbers had changed neither place nor posture, nor were they free from all emotion; impatience, fear, vexation and covetousness vanquished them by turns; they too had their reflections, they too had their sufferings to endure. One moment their thoughts wandered amid danger and infamy, presenting fearful visions of the gallows and of death; the next they brightened into a golden future, mad revelry, lewdness and debauchery.

"I thought I heard the voice of a man," said one of them; "what do you say about going up stairs?"

"Wait, wait, for a moment longer." "No, no; I'm certain there are only women, come; lads, up we go; up we go."

At that instant, Cambray struck a light, showing the way; breaking open the doors he rushed up stairs, followed by the others, and soon found himself at the chamber containing the women. Entering, Cambray received a violent blow with an iron poker from the servant Elizabeth McLellan.

However, the three inmates were soon seized by their throats, tied up in blankets, and placed under the surveillance of three of the robbers, while the remaining two pillaged the house. Mrs. Montgomery was in a faint the greater part of the time, but, coming to herself, she implored the man watching her, in accents that might have melted the heart of a tiger: "You look like a good man," said she, "oh! have pity on me, and do not hurt me." "No, no, I'm not a good man. I'm a wicked man, a very wicked man. Mathieu, have you found anything yet?"

"Tut, tut; silence; hold your tongue."

The robbers ransacked the whole house, emptied

the cupboards, bureaux and trunks, tossing and mixing everything, appropriating a large quantity of silver and articles of value which they carried off with them; after having taken the cruel precaution of rolling and tying up the women and the boy in carpets, in such a way, that it was impossible for them to get out without great exertion.

It was daylight when they left the house, and as they passed through St. John's gate, laden with their spoils, they encountered the men of the watch, returning from their posts, who permitted them to pass unchallenged.

Cambray and Mathieu were placed on trial for this crime (28th March, 1837), and upon the evidence of Waterworth, their accomplice, they were both found guilty. At the time this took place, Lemire had been transported, and Stewart was dead.

CHAPTER X.

An Expedition by Water—The Price of Indiscretion— A Critical Moment.

Some days after the robbery at Mrs. Montgomery's, two men might have been seen unrolling the sails of a small boat near the East India wharf; a third, standing on the wharf, said to one of them:

"Don't miss your chance, whatever you do; it's a matter of some consequence, as you know, and concerns our personal safety."

"Never fear, comrade, I'll do my share."

The sails were adjusted, and a moment after a light west wind carried the boat into the stream in the direction of the Island of Orleans.

It was on a beautiful evening in the month of June, a little before sunset; the shadows were deepening on the surface of the water, and the surrounding hills, fields and orchards, which Nature has grouped in such richness and variety in the vicinity of Quebec, were clad with verdure, and dotted with flocks, and the magnificent vessels from every portion of the globe reflected in the river—enhanced, if possible, the natural beauty of the scene. It was the fairy-like hour of enchantment, when the coming night lends her beauty and repose to the surrounding brilliancy, and day once more resumes its twilight of early purity. Deep in the crystal waters were the banks, the woods and the vessel masts reflected, and soft echoes of song from on board ship were wafted across them, and at intervals could be heard the distinct booming din of the neighbouring city.

But the breeze was stiffening; clearer and clearer sounded the rolling waves against the timbers of the fleet, and the moon, named by the ancients the chaste Lucinda—probably because she contemplates in silence the impurity and horror hidden from the day—rose gently through wind-driven clouds over the distant horizon.

Already the little yacht had cleared the almost inextricable labyrinth of vessels lying at anchor before the city, and now she was speeding across the basin between Quebec and the Island of Orleans, the lowering clouds were gathering in density, and the person on the wharf could see nothing but the sails; they appeared like a little white cloud skimming the roughening surface.

"You're very moody, this evening," said one of the sailors to his companion; "a good breeze this—a good breeze. I don't exactly know where you're taking me to; but this wind will carry us any distance. Tell me where is this timber you speak of? Is there much of it?"

"You'll know when we get there," replied the other savagely.

"Hallo!" muttered the first, "he's not in a good humour, it seems. I say, comrade, does what I said at Mrs. A.'s stick in your heart still? Listen now. I told nothing of consequence. I only said I knew those connected with the Montgomery affair—that's all. I mentioned no names; and as I was tipsy at the time, nothing can come of it."

"For goodness sake, don't speak of it," said the other passionately, repressing an angry movement, grinding his teeth, and trembling in every limb. "Now's the time I think; I'm far enough—yes, this is the place."

"What!" interrupted the first loquaciously, "is this your grapple—this big stone, with a couple of fathoms of cable; only one, that won't go very far, I think."

"Further than you are aware of, perhaps; but—but—look here. Devil take it, listen—quick—hurry yourself, or the sail will tear itself in two."

"And why did you let go? You had it in hand. Never mind—all for luck, I suppose. We're between the churches now. Are we going down the river?"

So saying, he threw himself into the fore-part of the boat; and, mounting on one of the seats, he bent over the side to catch the sail, which was flapping furiously in the wind, and which escaped as soon as caught. While occupied in this manner, his companion leaving the tiller, stole quietly to his side, and, seizing the rope attached to the grapple, which a moment before had excited so much derision, he threw the noose over the head of the unfortunate man, and before he had time to utter a single exclamation, with a sudden jerk he hurled him overboard into the seething billows. The wretch, who committed this, then seated himself quietly on the bulwarks, and watched with savage joy the bubbles rising from the water that had just closed over his victim. When, lo! at a short distance, and in the full light of the moon, he beheld the face of his adversary glaring at him above the waters; he had rid himself of the weight, and the waves were fast driving him to the boat. With heart furious with rage and despair, he seemed to rise through the waves like a monster of the sea. The other leaned over to grasp his victim once more, and accomplish the work he had begun. At last they met; the drowning man struggled convulsively for a grasp—his hands closed upon the neck of his murderer—closed with the iron hold of death—his eyes rolled in agony, his body writhed madly in the yielding element, and his tongue poured forth the imprecations of the damned.

"Coward! traitor! I have you now. Do your worst. I shall not drown alone; no, I shall

B

not drown alone! you cannot make me quit my hold—death alone has strength for that."

The murderer's voice was chol ed in a violent effort to give utterance to his feelings, his parched mouth moistened with blood, which a moment afterwards gushed forth in a torrent on the figure beneath him. Dreadful, indeed, became the struggle; he felt himself drawn gradually out of the boat, till his feet alone seemed inside. The other, curbed in his desperation by the approach of death, felt as if hanging by a thread over an unfathomable abyss—felt his life giving way—his hand slipping from its hold.

This scene of horror would probably have lasted some time, had not the wind now risen to a gale, driving the waves with such impetuosity against the boat as to positively raise the combatants and tear them asunder. The drowning man, thrown back once more, swam round and round, watching eagerly for an opportunity of renewing the contest; but it never came. All his efforts to regain his hold upon the boat were vain; his adversary, armed with an iron-shod gaff, struck him violently several times as he approached, till, completely exhausted, the unfortunate man rolled over into the surging billows, and disappeared from view.

A gleam of savage joy shot through the murderer's heart, throbbing wildly with the excitement and the triumph of the hour. Again he set the sails, and this time he was alone; again the boat darted like a bird over the bosom of the deep—again was the tide rising, and the moon, as though to congratulate him upon the victory, burst at that moment through the heavy clouds, and continued her silent course in the heavens. But scarcely had he run thirty fathoms when he perceived what appeared to be the head of a man caught in the stem of the boat; it seemed to look at him steadfastly for a moment, and then vanish as mysteriously as it had come. Unnerved by terror, the murderer shrank involuntarily from the sight. Again he turned towards it, and still the horrid phantom head appeared and disappeared as before.

In a paroxysm of rage at being thus haunted, he seized the gaff once more, and, approaching the object, he discovered it to be the dead body of his victim, which, by some unaccountable action of the water, had become fastened to the stem of the boat, and was thus towing ashore. Raising his arm, the iron hook of the gaff descended upon the skull, dashing out its brains with almost superhuman force; and as the detached body swept past, he yelled out:

"Go—go to the dead now, and tell them what you know. See if they'll listen to you."

In a few minutes he had reached the city, and stepping upon the wharf he had left the night before, he was met by the person who had seen them off.

"Well, what have you done?" asked he.

"What had to be. I had some trouble, though; but his affairs are settled—we are quit of him—his threats will no longer alarm us, for dead men tell no tales."

"Bravo! that's the way to serve traitors; but come along, and have something to eat, for, by my faith, you deserve it. Let's hear the story now, it will whet our appetites."

So saying they stepped into a tavern.

The man whose cruel death we have just recounted was James Stewart, whom we have already mentioned in connection with the Montgomery robbery. He paid dearly for a word dropped in a drunken spree; his murderers were——, but we shall withhold their names for the present.

———

CHAPTER XI.

The Montmorency murders—Cambray at the parsonage—A chattering housekeeper—The Sexton accused —The two Griffiths.

One evening, as the rain was falling in torrents and the darkness was so great that at the distance of three paces nothing could be seen, two farmers, from the Parish of Chateau Richer, on their return from market, arrived at a small ford a little above the Falls of Montmorency, when suddenly five bandits, armed with clubs and daggers, presented themselves, and, seizing them by their coat collars, accosted them with the terrible sentence : "Your money or your life."

"You must take our lives then, for we have no money," said one of them.

"Liar! I saw you receive fifty dollars on the market place not four hours ago: our boat has good sails, and we got here before you. Now do you understand—come out with it—out with it, or we'll take the sweat out of our sticks ; we'll knock the blood out of you."

The two farmers, trembling with fear, and far from any house where they could have obtained help, surrendered their purses. As one of them handed his to the man who held him, he leant forward with a movement of surprise, and exclaimed : "Why, Polette, is it you, and are you hard-hearted enough to assassinate the companion of your infancy, he with whom your younger days were spent, he who has saved your life twenty times by keeping your pranks secret?"

In truth he had recognised Mathieu among the brigands. Mathieu was a native of the Beaupré Hills, a redoubtable thief known by the name of Polette ; but ten years had elapsed since he had left his birthplace, and entered upon the more extended sphere of city life. He had become proud since then, was ashamed of his early plebeian life just as the clerk of a tavern in town looks down upon his brethren of the village.

"Ah, you know me," said Mathieu ; "ill luck betide you, 'tis your sentence of death. Had not your memory been so bright, you might have got away with only the loss of your money ; but now, if you live I shall be hung ; it must be your life or mine."

At that moment the five robbers drew the unfortunate men from their carts, threw them on the ground, and, dragging them into the water held them there until drowned. As soon as they were dead, they untackled their horses, pushed the carts into the stream, and threw the bodies in after them, in order that, when found, people would think they had missed the ford and fallen a prey to the accident. This accomplished, they went back to their boats, a distance of two leagues.

An hour later, about six o'clock in the evening, a man respectably clad, but drenched with rain, presented himself at the house of the Curate of Beaupré, asking whether he could have lodgings for the night. On his admission, his host cried out in accents of friendship:

"How, is it you, Cambray, and where are you going at such a rate? Come, you must have supper with me, and then I've an excellent bed for you."

"Oh, I'm not going far, only a shooting party to St. Ann's. But I shan't refuse your supper, for I've a splendid appetite."

Thus did they engage in conversation, laughing friendly and familiar, while a delicious and bountiful supper was being laid upon a little round table hard by, and in a few minutes the two friends were attacking it.

"Look there," said the curate, "look, there's a fire on the beach; more vagabonds I suppose, come to steal our sheep to-night."

"Pardon me, sir," said Cambray, "they are the sailors who brought me here; they will leave with the turn of the tide."

The two friends supped heartily, after which the curate took up his breviary, and Cambray went into the kitchen to dry his clothes at the chimney fire.

The curate had a housekeeper, and, like all curate's and bachelor's housekeepers, the woman had more tongue than discretion. Cambray soon got chattering with her, and in less than ten minutes he knew all the curate's affairs—how many sheep he had, how much money—where the keys were, where the sacred vases and papers of consequence, together with a goodly stock of village scandal and gossip. All this was told with an air of great importance, the old woman always speaking in the plural *we*. We did this —we did that, we desire that this shall be done so—we are of this opinion, myself and the curate.

And when every mystery had been ventilated, she conducted Cambray to his room, took her broth à la reine, and retired for the night.

Next morning terrible excitement reigned in the parsonage—people crying—running hither and thither, coming in, going out.

It appears the curate, on entering the church, previous to saying mass, noticed that the sacred vases had been stolen during the night. Cambray, *awakened* by the noise of the housekeeper, the servants, the singers and the sexton, dressed himself quickly and hastened to join in the bustle.

In the midst of this din he approached the curate and whispered softly in his ear, "By whom the church has been robbed I can't say— but I have seen a rather suspicious looking character in your kitchen; the man is fearfully agitated—I must confess, I don't like his appearance —there he is.'

"Eh, oh. Why, that's the sexton."

"The sexton, oh then, it can't be he. I suppose he does not keep the keys."

"No, but it is he who shuts the doors, returned the curate—still I think he's an honest man, its

true though, it's true, he seems greatly agitated, who can say?"

· That day the sexton was arrested and thrown into prison. The old housekeeper told all her neighbours how for a length of time she had had her suspicious of who the thief was—meantime, Cambray had joined his party in the boat.

"I've hooked the church plate," said he on arriving, "and more than that they've got the sexton in the *brig* (prison) for the job."

The robbers then went to "Isle aux Oies" where they assassinated the two unfortunate Griffiths, but why they did so, remains a mystery to the present hour. Three months later the poor sexton was tried for the church robbery and acquitted—he was innocent.

CHAPTER XII.

Murder of Captain Sivrac—Effrontery and temerity— The Skimmers—A reverse of fortune—Arrest of Cambray and Waterworth—The veil torn aside.

These, said Waterworth, resuming the recital we have interrupted for a moment by another form of narrative; these are the crimes in which I have taken part, and which continued without interruption from the month of November to the month of July, 1835.

I know there is another charge placed to our account, one on which Cambray was tried and acquitted before the Criminal Court, namely, the murder of Captain Sivrac.

Though Captain Sivrac gave the names of his assassins on his death bed, and though Cambray, since his conviction stated that he, I, and others were present at his murder, probably with the view of revenging himself on me and getting me into difficulty, I solemnly declare that I have never been at Lotbinière, and that I never imagined there was money to be found in the miserable hut occupied by Sivrac.

I have often, whilst in prison, heard the details of this affair, and know them to have been of a most revolting nature. A solitary and defenceless old man attacked upon an inhospitable island, severely beaten—forced by the most inhuman treatment to give up all he possessed, and to crown the barbarity after having beaten him almost to death, to throw him into a cellar full of water, and lock the door upon him, were acts the most frightful, the most diabolical that imagination can invent; it was doing harm for harm's sake, a pure delight in acts of brutality. This was altogether opposed to our plan of working. When people submitted with good grace, and did not seek to oppose us, we never ill-treated them, persuaded that it was more to our safety; that it would abate the rigour of pursuit and the danger of coming into contact with justice. It is an adopted opinion among robbers that the murderer never escapes death, and if this sentence was never pronounced but in such cases, I firmly believe that it would in a great measure do away with violence in burglarious attempts.

By this time we had quite forgotten the suspicions that had reached even our very doors, and we lived in the greatest possible security. Little did we think that the first rumor was as a snowball started from a mountain top, destined to gather size with every movement, till at last it descended with crushing violence upon its un-suspecting victims; but Cambray in his assu-rance thought to quell any storm that might arise by his effrontery and bravado.

The day after the robbery of the Congrega-tional Chapel he visited the place for the mere purpose of gratifying his vanity and audacious curiosity, and, passing by the Chapel with a friend, as though by accident, he got him to re-count all the details known concerning the mat-ter.

"Robbed the Chapel," said he, "and how did they get in? What, by this window! what audacity, what atrocity—to rob a church in the face of God himself, as one may say! It's horri-ble, horrible! it makes one's blood curdle to hear of it. They carried away the silver; but what will they do—what will become of them—it seems so incredible; but they have been some miserable prison birds, I suppose."

In making these edifying remarks he had en-tered the chapel with the guardian, and at each new revelation of pillage, he affected the utmost surprise and astonishment.

He did not hesitate to follow a like course with regard to all subsequent expeditions, and it must be allowed that, aided by this false sem-blance of honesty and his babblings of morality, for a length of time he succeeded in escaping the suspicions of the blind goddess of Justice.

But we went further than this in our measures of precaution, for we threatened, and even used violence where we deemed it necessary; and having thus foiled first suspicions, Cambray and I made arrangements to recommence our traffic in wood, to dupe the entire world, but espe-cially strangers who had possessed any money. These were seduced into hotels where, in the exercise of our lucrative and industrial talents, we rarely, if ever, failed in lightening them of their effects. There are, in several parts of this town, many houses of entertainment where from the host down to the servants in his employ, in-cluding a numerous fry of attachés, all reap con-siderable profit in the way we have mentioned.

I was not a little surprised to meet there fre-quently people who ranked by no means with the lower grades of society, people who pretend-ed to be gentlemen. They were adventurers, it is true, but they had the impudence to mix with honest people. They were rascals of the vilest stamp; one with hypocritical face played upon the best feelings of human nature, by preaching virtue, while his associate, more hardened or more skillful, was extracting the purse of the listener, or involving him in some game in which he was sure to be a loser to some extent.

We were on the high road to fortune when the avalanche fell; we were arrested and thrown into prison. In the records of the Court the de-tails of this unfortunate business will be found; it happened on a fine day in the middle of July, at about three o'clock in the afternoon. The evening before this certain magistrates furnished with an authentic document, had searched the premises occupied by Cambray, and taken there-from some silver spoons and a telescope. That day Cambray had spent the greater part of his time cockfighting in the *Palais*, according to his laudable custom.

On his arrival at home about the hour men-tioned, his wife, whom he found alone, for (Wa-terworth was absent), gave him in lengthy de-tail an account of the magisterial visit.

"Did they say nothing more—nothing *very* significant?" asked he, "did you read nothing striking in their demeanour? Did they often ask to see me?"

"But why so many questions concerning so tri-fling a matter, if as you told me yesterday morn-ing it is only a seizure for ten pounds, owed by Waterworth, for which you have become respon-sible, it can never ruin us; it but verifies the old proverb, ''he who answers pays.'"

"Well, you see it is because I do not think their mode of proceeding strictly legal. To en-ter a house as they did, seems to me rather a stretch of authority."

"Do not agitate yourself," replied the young woman, "there is nothing disgraceful in the matter: if it were even for your own debt, a promise of your own unfulfilled, it might then be a subject of trouble, of shame, but *security* only, there is no shame in that. Ah! Heavens, what do I see? Look there! look, they are speaking together and pointing to the house—now they are coming towards it. Oh, have you concealed anything from me? What do they want? What *can* they want? Let me lock the door."

"Stop, stop! no foolery," replied her husband with affected coolness, and rising from his chair with a firm step, he crossed the room and lay down upon the sofa. While this conversation was going on, an acute observer might have no-ticed a certain embarrassment in his manner and speech; doubt, even fear, at times flitted across his countenance, as if disturbed by some secret presentment. In truth, when his wife pronounc-ed to him the terrible words, "here they are," he made an involuntary bound from where he was, a cold shiver seemed to pass over him, and for a moment he remained pale, immovable and de-jected. "Can it be" muttered he between his teeth, "can it be that we are discovered, betray-ed?"

Coming to himself again, his strength of mind once more resumed its sway, he became calm and collected, seemed to despise his ill-fortune, and resolved to brave his destiny; when suddenly the house resounded to a thundering knock, and five or six men, among whom were several mem-bers of the constabulary, entered and surround-ed him with dreadful precision.

"What do you desire, gentlemen?" said Cam-bray, in affected unconcern, rising from the sofa and crossing his arms arrogantly over his chest.

"In the name of the King, you are my prison-er," said one of the magistrates, placing his hand upon Cambray's shoulder and signalizing the others to seize him.

"What do you mean? Why am I arrested?"

"Why, Cambray, you are accused of murder. Do you remember *Sivrac*? You are accused of sacrilege. Were you never in the Congrega-tional Chapel? Have you not stolen silver in your possession? Is the name of Cecelia O'Con-nor unknown to you? These are the grounds upon which you are arrested."

Cambray, always cool and collected, cast his

eyes on the warrant for his arrest, and while it was being read, he became paler and paler at every word ; nevertheless he maintained his composure throughout the entire proceedings, looking stedfastly in the face of the magistrate.

"Sivrac was my friend," said he at length, with an evident effort to restrain himself; but suddenly losing all patience, he stamped upon the floor, exclaiming, " but what is the use of all this ? is it thus you speak to a free and innocent man ? When you bring me before justice, I will laugh at your accusations."

During the first part of this speech his face became livid and his eyes fairly flashed with fury, but he soon masked himself with innocence and confidence ; an expression of mockery gleamed in his eyes and curled upon his lips ; one would have said that he already had a foretaste of the joy of seeing his enemies confuted in their assertions.

On the appearance of the magistrates, his wife had retired into another apartment, but her interest in the ordeal to which her husband was submitting, was too great not to listen to it all.

"Well then, come," said Cambray, "Come, come ! let us see whether or not I am the murderer of Sivrac. Come !" and as he was preparing to depart, his wife burst shrieking into the room and threw herself towards him. Pale, trembling, her hair falling loosely over her shoulders, it was with difficulty she could respire. Mute with terror at the thoughts of his sufferings, and anticipating his despair, with imploring eyes she turned to those surrounding him ; thrice did she try to find words to give utterance to her feelings, but agony had deprived her of her voice. At last a shriek burst from her pent up heart—but such a shriek—it was scarcely human, so wild was it, so touching, and so full of anguish.

"Ah, what do I see? What do I hear? What are you going to do with him ?" cried she.

For a moment there was a deep silence. Cambray alone had sufficient energy to bear it. He raised her with affected solemnity, and said, "My wife, rouse yourself, be courageous, and show yourself worthy of your husband ; remember you are the partner of one who never quailed in the presence of man ; remember that and fear nothing. You know me well ; now listen. I am accused of a crime, a most dreadful crime— that of murder—but an accusation is no proof of guilt."

These terrible words sounded like a death knell in the ears of his distracted wife, who fell back into the arms of a neighbour who had entered the house attracted by the noise. Cambray alone appeared unaffected by the mournful sight, and marched bravely to the prison, surrounded by the magistrates, and exposed to the jeers of the passers by, or the observations of those who hung out of the windows of their houses attracted by the unusual spectacle.

That evening Cambray was confronted with his accusers, and thrown into the lock-up. Shortly afterwards Waterworth, his associate, delivered himself into the hands of the authorities, resolved to share his fate whatever it might be.

So long as Cambray hoped to impose upon the public, by assuming an apparent indifference, so long did he appear quiet and submissive ; but

no sooner did he discover that the veil had been torn aside from his iniquitous career—no sooner did he learn the damning array of evidence against him, than he gave way to the wildest transports of rage.

During the first part of his confinement he was morose, at times ferocious and brutal in his bearing, so much so that even the witnesses who were to depose against him trembled in his sight. Not that he was afraid of death, nor ashamed of the infamous life he had been leading. No ; what troubled him was, that he had been short in his hey day of success.

Cambray and Waterworth, before "this reverse of fortune," as they were pleased to term it, were people of great distinction among their friends, and were generally respected by all who knew them. The following is an account by Waterworth, who resided the greater part of the year in town, of the manner in which affairs were conducted in Cambray's house for some time before his arrest.

It is astonishing, said he, to what an extent hypocrisy and position operate on the minds of the most worthy of our citizens, and it is remarkable that the first breath of suspicion comes generally from a quarter where it is least looked for ; it seems as if vice clashes with vice for the sole purpose of protecting society from universal corruption. Only a few days before our arrest, Cambray's house was the resort of people of the highest respectability. It will doubtless seem strange to you that one of his most intimate acquaintances was a person of most exemplary manners and conduct, one moreover whose position alone was a guarantee of respectability. This person could never have known the real character of his friend ; indeed from positive knowledge I can affirm, that he regarded Cambray as a model of honesty and truthfulness; alas like many others he was only a dupe ; under the genial smile of friendship lay a depth of villany, he would have recoiled from with horror.

The religious disposition of Cambray's wife did much towards bringing this class to the house, and it must be added that the cordial manners of her husband did much towards inducing them to repeat their visits. He did not however partake of the religious feelings of his spouse, for he possessed none, but he believed that the friendship and good opinion of his neighbours was likely to be useful to him ; consequently he aped the virtue others applauded.

I do not wish to insinuate that Cambray did not believe in the existence of a God ; far from this, his conduct proves the contrary, for in our iniquitous conspiracies he never failed to invoke the aid of the devil, and those who believe in an evil spirit, necessarily acknowledge a good one. The miserable wretch whose life has been dedicated to Satan, and who finds his death bed a scene of utter despair, proves the existence of one who has filled the heart of man with repentance and sorrow.

As I have already stated, we were enjoying the height of prosperity at the time of our arrest : fortune, fame and security seemed to wait at our doors, but the day of retribution had come, suspicion had fallen upon us, and in a moment all our bright hopes of the future had perished. No sooner were we taken up, than the most horrible of crimes, real or imaginary, were placed to our account, and the town accepting every detail as truthful, re-echoed with wrath and indignation ; thousands priding themselves upon their perspicuity or upon their pretended discoveries circulated the most ridiculous stories concerning our secret doings in all of which we were represented as the most atrocious monsters under Heaven. The guilty too loaded us with their own misdeeds, thus hoping to escape the vengeance that belonged to them.

This unfortunate piece of business suddenly opened our eyes to the enormities of our crime ; nevertheless we did not despair of escaping the rigor of the law, and of re-entering society once more, trusting that our full purses would make amends for our lost characters.

CHAPTER XIII.

First Night in the "Lock-up"—Reproaches—Criminal Reflections.

So far we have seen vice triumphant, marching with head erect, and in full defiance of justice. Here our subject changes colour a little, thoughts of the past arise, and fears for the future. Let us follow our characters in their defeat, listen to the clanking of their chains, and the imprecations of their fate.

We have unfolded the revolting details of their numerous crimes ; let us now unfold the consequences thereof, and witness the tribulation of their subsequent life. We have traced them from their first offence to the depth of their villainy ; let us now judge of their humiliation and punishment ; for who can paint repentance and remorse ?

On the evening of their arrest, Cambray and Waterworth were chained up in the same place. Behold them, one opposite the other, fastened by massive chains to the thick walls of the cell, wet with moisture and covered with cobwebs ; a lamp hangs between them, and its pale and sickly light seems to regard them with a restless and defiant glare.

Their forms are languid now and relaxed, and the pervading silence, interrupted by the sighs of one and the mutterings of the other, manifests more strongly than could word or gesture the nature of their thoughts. Had any one looked into this dungeon through the only aperture that admitted daylight—had seen their flaming eyes amid the gloom—they would have believed them to have been two ferocious brutes crouched in their respective corners, each trembling in the fear of being assailed by his adversary.

" See," said Waterworth, raising his chains, which sounded with a deep clank in this subterraneous abode. " See," said he, breaking at last the oppressive silence of the place, " what I owe you, Cambray ; see what you have brought me to."

" Ah ! you open your eyes at last ; I'll bet you are sorry for what you have done," replied Cambray, with a mocking laugh, as he gathered himself into a sitting posture.

" Heavens ! what will my father say when he hears of this ? What will he think ? What will

he do ? O that I had never seen you ! Cambray, it was you who enticed me to commit the acts I have done—you who deceived me—you alone are responsible."

" What would you say, you miserable coward ?" cried Cambray, throwing himself towards Waterworth as far as his chains would allow. " Would you reproach me ? Hold your tongue, or I'll strangle you with my chains ; hold your tongue, or I'll bury you in curses ; hold your tongue, or I'll call hell to my aid. What ! does it follow that because you were more timid than I, that you were less guilty ? And you wish to desert me, do you ? You wish to be my accuser. Is treason already on your lips ! Remember, I will not remain in chains forever. Choose, then, between secrecy or death."

" Cambray," said Waterworth, quickly, " you are unjust. I will not flinch, even in the presence of death itself, if by it I can save you. You know the truth of what I say—you know that I could swear to it ; but would it not have been better, had there been no necessity for this ? Ah, my friend, I have followed you in a career of crime ; and if fate wills it, I shall die with you."

" Bah—die—bah ! That may do for fools. What have we to fear ? Has not luck protected us so far through what you have the weakness to call ' a career of crime,' but what I would call the road to fortune, fame, and honour. It is true our star is somewhat eclipsed, and that we are rather unlucky for the time. It is certainly bad enough to be under suspicion ; but let us stand up like men, and battle bravely, and we'll soon rid ourselves of the trouble.

" The blow that levelled us came from Broughton ; it was your family that betrayed us ; had you taken my advice, you would have dispatched them long ago. Little, indeed, were you adapted for the part assigned you."

" Listen while I am able to tell you the object of my intentions, for I have never unfolded all. The veil is torn asunder ; now we are alone, and can speak freely, for the walls of our prison are discreet, and I have no reason to hide my thoughts from you. Listen, then, and learn to know me. I have felt what it is to be poor, Waterworth ; I have even been on the verge of starvation ; I have experienced the pride and disdain of the rich ; and I said to myself, reputation, happiness and fame are only the results of wealth. I said this ; and since then, surrounded by my fellows in misery, and with but a very limited circle of acquaintances, I have never felt the sting of poverty. Why ? Because, since then, the world at large has been my treasury from the entire human race. I have drawn my profits. Had I submitted to their laws, I might have died from hunger ; but, as their enemy, I have triumphed over everything. Live and enjoy yourself is the only law I know ; it matters not at whose expense. True it is that you now behold me stopped for the time in the glorious career I have pursued, enclosed between these four walls, and accused of crimes that may lead me perhaps to the scaffold. You weep—you tremble at the thought. Well, for my part, I laugh at it. I've plenty of courage yet ; and what is better, plenty of gold—gold, Water-

worth. I can buy up my jailors, break my
chains, and escape. I can have the best of
counsel, and the most powerful pleaders, so that
I may safely look forward to the day of liberation, when I may again commence with new
hopes and strengthened vigour."

" Do they know everything ?" interrupted
Waterworth ; " have they discovered all ?"

" No ; I think not. I have questioned them
thoroughly, and I believe I have arrived at the
nature of their evidence—mere trifles—dreams
based in a great measure upon their imaginations. The affairs of Parke and Sivrac ; that's
all."

" Sivrac ! What, that frightful murder !
Heavens ! you were not there ?"

" Oh, indeed, I was not there—was I not ?
True, true—an alibi, an alibi. Devil grant it, I
am saved. You can prove an alibi, can't you ?"

" I do not know ; I—I was not always with
you."

" What ! traitor !—do you hesitate ! Are you
too scrupulous to save the life of a friend—the
friend who has fed and clothed you—who
opened to you all the enjoyments of life at a
time when you wanted even its necessities.
Well may you cast down your head. Hear me,
Waterworth. Choose between my hate and
my gold. Will you swear it or not ?"

" I will swear anything, everything, Cambray. I feel like a child in your hands. There
is something about you—what, I know not—
that holds me faster than even the demon spirits
that have besieged my soul. I have heard that
there are certain wild animals that charm their
prey ; the power you have over me is stronger
still. You are so determined. But let us not
speak of what has passed ; these walls may hide
spies, for aught we know. I do not like to
think of such scenes of horror immediately before sleep ; my dreams frighten me. Heavens !
what a night we have passed ! What has fate
in hand for us ? Tell me not that man is master
of his own actions ; what has brought me to this
condition, if not fate ? Fate chains us to her
chariot wheels, and all are crushed in turn.
From birth I must have been singled out for
crime and eternal damnation."

" Such is your story," said Cambray, " and
here is my moral : It is absolute folly to commit
crime, and then throw the blame on another or
on Fate ; the fault remains with ourselves. Had
I wished I need never have been better than a
mere nincompoop ; but what others respected, I
defied—what others worshipped, I have trampled
under foot—and yet I have lived upon their
gains. Such are my principles—such my desires. I could have acted differently, but I did
not choose to."

" Is there anything more doleful, more melancholy, than the call of the sentinel every
quarter of an hour," said Waterworth ; " how
can I sleep with the voice of the persecutor ring-
ing in my ears ?"

" It is unpleasant," said Cambray ; " but let's
have a little music, to drive away melancholy,"
and he began to sing and shake his chains with
such violence, that the jailor, who was going
his rounds for the last time that night, rushed
to their cell, crying out " Ho, there," and threat-

ening to separate them—to put each in a different and dark cell—if they did not stop their
noise.

By the time all within this abode of crime
had relapsed into silence, two new arrivals made
their appearance ; they stretched themselves on
the cold and wet stone floor, and in a short time
all were fast asleep.

Next day Cambray's wife paid him a visit.
He spoke to her through the massive grated
door of his prison. She was very pale, and
greatly changed in appearance since he had
seen her—completely crushed with grief, and
resigned to the Divine will.

At the time of her husband's arrest she had
fainted, and her recovery was looked upon as
uncertain ; but her habitual suffering, hope,
and above all, the astonishing elasticity of character with which she was endowed, finally re-
established the calmness of her mind.

In this interview the horror of his situation
recalled the fearful thoughts of the past. No
longer able to control herself, she burst into
tears, sobbing violently.

Providence, in uniting this young, mild and
virtuous woman with a miserable bandit, ac-
corded her the privilege of succumbing to her
sufferings—of resigning a poisoned existence.
She died several months after the imprisonment of her husband.

CHAPTER XIV.

Life within the prison. The patriarch of thieves, or
Captain Dumas—several attempts at escape—the
German baron Van Kœing—the Jailer.

Cambray and Waterworth, several days after
their arrest, were taken out of the lockup and
placed in a room with about a dozen other
scoundrels in accordance with the deplorable
custom adopted in our prisons : there they met
Mathieu and Gagnon and several other villains
alike distinguished in the annals of vice. With
these they entered into criminal compacts and
fresh conspiracies against society. It is difficult
to imagine, and far more to portray the diabolical
manners that reigned in that lawless circle. To
give a faint idea of it, however, we shall again
adopt the language of the King's evidence Waterworth, from whom the greater part of our in-
formation has been derived.

" Whilst in the lock-up and loaded with chains,
our condition became so frightful to me that I
believe I could not have endured it much longer,
but as good luck would have it we were soon
taken out and placed in a room were we met
several of our old acquaintances. From this
day the prison by no means appeared so horrible
a place ; and had it not been for our natural
yearnings for liberty, a sentiment common to all
mankind and a subject of deep despair to the
inmates, we would have been rather happy than
otherwise. We had nothing to do all day but
to relate our former prowess and invent schemes
of escape and future depredations. Our ancient
friends told us of all their tricks, their adventures, their insight into the constructions of the
wealthiest houses and the projects in which they
expected to engage on their re-entrance into

the world. In this way we encouraged each other in vice, and the least experienced among us soon acquired a wondrous knowledge of our art. We had amongst us a singular character in the profession, one Dumas, an extremely expert and cautious thief, who though he had never incurred the risk of dancing in the air, he nevertheless had passed the greater part of his life in prison. By his companions, this man was called Captain Dumas, who looked up to him as their patriarch and instructor. This original character had kept a journal of his exploits and those of his little band for ten years, and also undertook the task of teaching the young the secret of his trickery, and of initiating the inexperienced into the details of criminal attempts past and future. At the approach of the criminal term, he nominated himself president of an Amateur Court, before which each of the prisoners pleaded his cause, to each he gave the substance of his defence, wrote speeches for them, addressed the jury, administered a paternal reprimand to the guilty, and laughingly pronounced sentence upon all. Thus the inmates mutually instructed each other in their little industrial vocations, and became familiar with the penalties imposed by the law on their misdemeanours. Among us was a man of herculean strength, who amused us by playing at hanging; this he did by suspending himself by the chin on a silk handkerchief and imitating the contortions of the body, while on the gibbet. We were not always idle, however; for while Mathieu busied himself in making keys of wood to carry out our projects of escape, Cambray and I had made arrangements with a coiner, named K——y, and in concert with him we worked at an apparatus, intended on our discharge, to convert our virgin silver into American half dollars.

One dark and rainy night, just such a one as invites the drowsy sentinel to a nap in his box, while it favours the enterprise of crime, we all set to work in right good earnest, to effect our escape. In a short time eight doors had been opened, a ceiling pierced, a wall broken through, a rope ladder hung; all that was wanted to complete our liberation was the signal " are you ready," when the ill-omened voice of alarm sounded through the jail, and we were discovered.

Immediately a picket of soldiers invested the place, and we all rushed to our beds to escape the punishment consequent upon the attempt. It is astonishing that it is almost impossible to enter into any conspiracy without a rumor of it reaching the ears of the jailer; there are too many people in the same apartment, there is always some traitor to be found among them, who to gain favour is ready to sacrifice the lives of his companions; but we well knew how to punish these treasonable disclosures and carefully watched the suspected spy, making him pay dearly for any little favours he obtained. Cambray above all was inexorable in his persecution, till at last the jailer was compelled to remove some of his victims, who till that time had lived in perpetual martyrdom.

During the time I remained in prison, there were several attempts of this nature, the most daring of which was perhaps that of Cambray. One day whilst we were all in the yard the door was opened to permit the entrance of a load of wood. Cambray, seizing the opportunity, rushed through the gate into the street, overturning a carter in his violence, together with a sentry, who stood on guard, but his precipitation was checked by the vehicle, and he was retaken by some soldiers who had arrived in time to prevent his escape. But the best concerted plan took place shortly after this event.

One of the prisoners—and it was Mathieu, we believed, who had taken this liberty—had made wooden keys for every door of the jail not excepting even that of the entrance. Every arrangement had been made for a general sortie, and the conspirators were completely sheltered from suspicion. Prevost, who was at the head of this movement, was to have opened the doors of every room during the night time, gathered the prisoners in the passage, descended quietly and opened the outer door, given the signal to leave, got the whole band noiselessly into the passage, armed the most determined with the guns of the guard, and led them all into the street, with the full determination to assassinate the sentinel had he offered to oppose their exit. This plan was partly carried into effect, and whilst the little army was arranged in the passage, awaiting impatiently the signal of Prevost, who was a criminal condemned to transportation and who had descended to open the doors, he, in order to have his sentence commuted, informed the jailer and thus made a merit of his treason, and obtained great favour for having done so, while the least guilty in the affair were thrown into the cells. This Prevost is a man of the very worst character; he fully merits transportation, and I heartily hope it may come to pass before long.

Our companions in this abode of crime were men entirely lost to decency and character; but sometimes hatred or predudice or blind suspicion threw the innocent or the young in with the rest. It was horrible to listen to the sarcasm and jesting of which these simpletons, for so we called them, were made the subjects; and if the new comers were not proof against every thing in the shape of vice, the contagion of evil in every form, they were sure to fall into the ways of those by whom they were surrounded.

There is a man there at present of high birth and great honesty. I am convinced that he was reduced to the greatest misery by a series of misfortunes, and by deplorable accident he was finally thrown into this den of infamy. He was an inhabitant of St. Jean Port Joly, a Canadian peasant. He was known in his parish as the German Baron, a local corruption of Van Kœing, which in the German signifies son of the King. He told me his history: it is one of great interest, even romantic in its details. His father was an officer in an English regiment, which was stationed in Canada about sixty years ago; he was of German parentage, being the only son of Baron Van Kœing, one of the most noble and wealthiest Barons of Germany. His father placed him in the English army until such time as his age warranted his appearance among the dignitaries of his native Empire. Unfortunately this young officer, amiable, wealthy and with every prospect of fame before him, was naturally of a thoughtless disposition, preferring a life of contented retirement to the labour and anxiety attendant upon a distinguished position. Having wandered over the greater part of Canada, he at last fixed his residence at " Riviere Ouelle " where he became acquainted with a beautiful peasant girl, the daughter of a farmer in that vicinity, whom he afterwards married.

For some time he lived in plenty and never dreamed of returning to Germany, but his resources soon began to fail, his family to increase, his pledges of affection to double, and this son of the king saw the moment of indigence rapidly approaching. At last his father's death occurred and the succession became vacant ; too poor and too idle to reclaim his estates in person, the German Baron employed a Canadian lawyer in his stead, giving him power to dispose of his domains and dignities. The collateral inheritors, who, in the absence of the heir, had succeeded to the immense property, to disencumber themselves of the legitimate claimant gave his agent a sum of several thousand florins, quite sufficient to render the Canadian family of Van Koeing perfectly independent, but which was completely squandered at the end of twenty years. The son of this Baron destined by birth to revel in luxury, to hold dominion over his fellow creatures, to adorn the foremost ranks of society in Europe, found himself at more than thirty years of age, poor, ignorant, humble in appearance as the peasantry with whom he had been brought up, and to crown all, the inmate of a prison. Where then is the superiority of birth and rank ? —raise the democrat, the man of the people, and lower the monarch, and not one of nature's laws will be broken, not a principle violated.

You are aware that last winter the inhabitants of the various parishes of the county of Rimouski and Kamouraska were reduced to great want by the failure of their crops. St. John Port Joly suffered considerably in the general dearth, and among the rest the German Baron found himself, his wife and children, on the verge of starvation.

One fearfully cold evening, when the thermometer stood at fifty degrees below zero, and the wind beat furiously over the village and against the frozen woods in the vicinity, there was neither food nor firewood in the Baron's house, and his half naked family, faint with hunger and shivering with cold, hung weeping around their master, imploring to get them a little bread. Grief and despair in his heart, he left the house in the middle of the night and cautiously made his way to the house of a rich neighbor, and returned with a loaf of bread and a few pounds of pork. The following day being suspected be was arrested for the act, and thrown into prison, where he has remained for three months awaiting his trial without being able to find bail for his re-appearance.

The history of the German Baron is only one among thousands of the same kind, equally interesting and instructive.

I have now been some time shut up in this prison—continued Waterworth—and I have keenly felt the privation of freedom, but I must acknowledge that we have ever been indebted to the jailer for his sympathy and humanity in ameliorating our unfortunate condition. Notwithstanding the vexations to which he was constantly exposed by the ill temper of some of the inmates, and the general inconvenience resulting from the various arrangements of the building, he was ever in good humour and omitted no means of rendering our lives as supportable as circumstances would permit ; mildness and firmness act much more favourably than would severity, which only aggravates the evil passions of the perverse and inflexible.

Do not imagine, however, that there is any looseness in our discipline ; on the contrary it requires all the vigilance of our jailer to watch the treachery that is daily being woven around him, and to control so great a number of prisoners within so small space. For all have constant intercourse with outsiders, who furnish them with the necessary instruments to effect escape, and generally aid them in carrying out their nefarious schemes.

" Scarcely a day passses in which confiscations are not made—of keys, cords, knives and aquafortis,'and all the various et ceteras required for that purpose—these are enclosed in baskets by officious sweethearts, longing for the delivery of their beloved, who draw them up to the windows by means of cords.

CHAPTER XV.

Waterworth's reasons for turning King's Evidence— Correspondence between Cambray and Waterworth on this subject.

In the course of these revelations, Waterworth has not given any reason for having turned King's evidence against his associates, and it became necessary to use much persuasion in order to induce him to speak of it, for it seemed as though he reproached himself for the act. At last, however, he consented, and it was thus he explained the fact :

" I had been in the lock-up several days for some trick I had been guilty of, and during that time I experienced all the horror of isolation ; my days were occupied in giving way to the most violent transports of rage, and my nights by frightful dreams.

" I fancied I saw figures tracing my death sentence on the walls around me, or busily employed in erecting my scaffold.

" One day when I had exhausted myself in one of my fits of desperation, and felt as if all the energies of life had departed, the jailer paid me a visit, and informed me that Cambray had had an interview with the officers of the Crown, and had volunteered to reveal the true details of our criminal career, on condition of being set at liberty on the expiration of the Criminal Term in September (1836), and of receiving pardon for his share in the matter.

" ' He stipulated,' said the jailer, ' above all to have his freedom without any delay whatever.' This led me to suspect his real motive in saying, as he did on one occasion, ' We have large sums of money in reserve—as yet we have not touched the Congregational silver '—and it was doubtless Cambray's intention to come out snugly, and sacrifice me for the purpose of being able

to take entire possession of our mutual gains.
'Well, since I have been betrayed, I am delivered from my oaths. I must be before them.'

"On that day, without any condition whatever, I offered my declaration to the officer of the Crown, and my offer was accepted. I do not know whether I was the victim of any trickery, but this I know that Cambray swore revenge to the death for my having played him such a trick.

"As we were kept in separate apartments we were obliged to write to each other. This we often did. Our correspondence generally turned on projects of escape, or new expedients proposed by Cambray, with the view of getting out of our trouble. The following, however, I received last autumn :

' Waterworth!
' You have sworn by the Devil to keep our secrets. You have broken your oath, you have turned King's evidence, you stand dishonoured before all your associates as having eaten your own words. For that act you well know I have the right to kill you. Think not that because I and others are now enchained between four walls you can escape my vengeance. When I desire it I can find a subterraneous passage to your cell and strangle you; but you know I have ever been your friend, and I have now the means of saving us both. I am only accused of theft, —the murder of Sivrac is yet unpunished,—let us like two brothers, you and I, bear witness against some of the ragamuffins in this place, against P—— or G—— if you like.

' You see by this means we shall both be saved, for the murder of Sivrac was an abominable affair, one that I almost regret, for not one *sou* did I put in my pocket. As soon as I am once free you shall have half of my hidings.

' I must tell of a good precautionary trick I have taken. About twenty rascals have lately left the *brig* (prison), and I succeeded in speaking to them. They intend assaulting everybody in the streets by way of revenge. This will have the effect of diverting attention from us and throwing the indignation of the public upon them, you see.

' It's a pity you have betrayed me, but I may yet make a large fortune. Write me if you are willing to arrange matters concerning Sivrac's affair ; if not, I shall have your life.
            CAMBRAY.'

" To this I replied somewhat as follows :
' Cambray !
' You reproach me with having violated my obligations and of betraying my associates, but it is from you I have taken example, and now you propose fresh treason, still more contemptible, for it is founded on falsehood.

' For a length of time you have deceived me, representing fortune and pleasure as the reward of brigandage ; you have taken advantage of your influence over me, and made me the instrument of your cupidity ; but I have arisen from this dream—my eyes are open—yes, I will be King's evidence, not against the innocent whom you would charge with the murder of Sivrac, but against you, Cambray ; and you will see when my recital is made whether or not my memory is a faithful one.

' You must be an incarnate devil to boast of having engaged the miserable wretches who were set at liberty to attack people in the street, in order to divert public attention from yourself. You ask my motive for acting thus, here is my answer—
' The devil told me I was doing well,
   And afterwards that my deeds were chronicled in
     hell.'   .   .

Such is the case now—I am no longer under your influence, and I believe I need not respect the criminal oaths I have taken any longer. For this reason I shall reveal everything. I laugh at your threats and your impotent wrath. Rely no longer upon me.   WATERWORTH.'

" It was not without considerable effort that I resolved upon sending this desperate answer to my comrade, from whom in return I received the following reply :
' Waterworth!
' We will yet meet, in a cell, in a narrow passage, on the scaffold, perhaps, or at any rate in hell—no matter where ; but so surely as you fall into my hands I'll choke you—I'll massacre you. Meantime I send you my direst curses, thou infamous traitor.   CAMBRAY.'

" At last the March Assizes (1837) came ; Cambray and his accomplices were placed upon trial, and I rendered evidence in the matter. I must admit when I was confronted with my former comrades my heart revolted at my position, and remorse followed on the footsteps of truth.

" Alas I wish I could see Cambray before I leave. I would not be afraid to meet him for he is unarmed. We could not behold each other without emotion, I am certain.

" But here I must be allowed to terminate this recital, to draw a veil over these sad events, for the remainder is known to you all."

Some days after this (6th April, 1837,) Waterworth was set at liberty, and left for ever, to seek his fortune elsewhere.

CHAPTER XVI.

Trial of Cambray and Mathieu — Conviction and Sentence—The First Night of the Condemned.

During the long and interesting trial undergone by Cambray and Mathieu for the robbery committed at Mrs. Montgomery's, and of which we have given the full details, the accused, seated in the criminal dock, overlooking the crowd, remained perfectly calm and collected, regarding from time to time with much assurance and an unfaltering eye, witnesses, judges, and jury, and casting at times disdainful or threatening glances at certain personages among the crowd. Mathieu, especially, appeared imperturbably cool, while his accomplice, Cambray, more capable of feeling the humiliation of his position, was, to judge from his convulsive efforts to repress his emotions, violently agitated. Not that fear or remorse had aught to do with these sensations—rage and disappointment alone were the cause of all his pangs. The sufferings he had experienced in prison were deeply graven on his countenance, slight contractions about his mouth marked infallibly the anguish and mental torture he had endured, and effaced in some measure his affected serenity ; and he, who had been so remarkable for manly vigour and joyousness, now appeared ill in health and shattered in constitution. Notwithstanding that his guilt was manifest to all present, still more than one gazed on him with expressions of sincere compassion, while the more timid and simple, looking upon a man above the stamp of vulgarity, admired the apparently unwavering fortitude with which he comforted himself.

On Waterworth's entering the box to bear witness against them, they stood up and glared at him with eyes of fire, looking as if they wished to penetrate to the inmost depths of his heart. But the denouncer was prepared for this encounter, for he raised his eyes to Cambray calmly and collectedly, and, having gazed on him for a moment, without evincing the least emotion, he turned to the Court, and gave his testimony fearlessly and with precision: it was evident he had made up his mind to unveil the whole, so resigned and open his confession. Nevertheless the struggle with his nature was severe ere he could reconcile himself to this act of treachery, still the tenor of his conversation was not tinged with that remorse or confusion that so frequently forms the substratum of feeling in the hearts of the guilty, even where every other sentiment of honour has been abandoned.

The evidence went sorely against the accused ; the only defence that Cambray's counsel could make was reduced to a question of credulity on the part of the accomplice. Mathieu's counsel asked Mrs. Montgomery if, when she heard the name of Mathieu pronounced, it was not possible that it might have been intended for some other person than the prisoner, from which arose the question whether it was not a fact that the name was a common one.

The jury retired, and re-entered immediately, amid the most universal anxiety on the part of all present. Everybody, but especially the prisoners, tried to read the verdict in their faces. There was a moment of deep silence, and then came the fatal sentence :

" Charles Cambray and Nicolas Mathieu are guilty of the crimes of which they stand accused."

Mathieu, on hearing the verdict, showed no emotion whatever : neither restraint nor embarrassment indicated the least affectation of calmness.

Cambray, on the contrary, appeared for the moment violently agitated and despairing—a thousand thoughts rushed through his mind, and weighed upon his imagination.

Their trial was over, and they were brought back to prison, surrounded by a crowd of people.

Cambray, who was ill at the time, pretended that he was too weak to walk, and was therefore conducted in a vehicle.

Several days after this their sentence of death was pronounced with imposing solemnity by the president of the Court, in tones of pity, and in the presence of an expectant but silent multitude of spectators.

The prisoners bore up against the terrible ordeal with firmness and resolution. Cambray maintained a proud and disdainful mien, but, raising his head, several great tears coursed down his cheeks—tears it would be difficult to say whether of weakness or regret. Mathieu was also at his ease, as much as if he had not had the slightest interest in the event ; he amused himself by playing with his hands upon the dock, a spectacle which on another occasion would have appeared insignificant or ridiculous, but which on the present left a sad and painful impression on the minds of all who witnessed it.

The first night of the condemned was one of depression, horror, and mental agony too great either to paint or analyse. Who can inspire the healthy and hopeful with an idea of the desolation experienced by the unfortunate being whose existence is measured by the near approach of death—death branded with infamy, and within an allotted period ? Every movement, every thought, every nervous quiver, is to him a step towards the end of his existence, a thread diminished to the cord of existence, and added to that which is destined to launch him into eternity—a voice calling on him to efface the judgment by appearing before his Creator.

Ever before his eyes are walls grated and silent—livid light—enormous doors—guardians —chains—the hangman—and, finally, infamy and death—death—a frightful spectre, which every one has gazed upon, and which every one must experience, and yet the existence of which all appear to doubt, but which the condemned felon is alone destined to meet face to face. Death is already standing before him, inexorable and inflexible.

Such is the fate of the unhappy being upon whose head the sentence has fallen—the dread certainty within a known time doubles and triples his agony of mind. Had he even the power of convincing himself of the justice of the sentence ? but, alas ! from the depths of his heart the cry of despair comes to him in the accents of rage. Man,—has he a right to take away human life ?—boldest thou not thine from the Creator alone ? Thus does he disclaim against society, in spite of crime, and is ushered on to the scaffold, his heart burning with hatred and vengeance. Such is an approximation to the feelings experienced by Cambray and Mathieu, modified by the individuality of each. Cambray's conduct was that of a ferocious beast bounding about in frenzy, shaking chains, yelling, dashing himself down, till, overpowered by exertion, he became calm and reflective, ferreting his brains for expedients to gain sympathy, and, if possible, to lull the storm once more.

Mathieu, more resigned to his condition, and less violent in disposition, retained his calmness and serenity. He nourished no thought of escaping the gibbet, and regarded it as the natural consequence of his crimes.

In the course of forty-eight hours the greater part of their sufferings were over. The elasticity of the mind, that which gives strength and energy to the human character, which familiarises us with every situation, and supports us in the greatest trouble, gradually restored calmness to the minds of our heroes, and permitted them to spend the day with some degree of indifference, and the night in deep repose. However, both Cambray and Mathieu requested an interview with some minister of religion. Mathieu had a Catholic priest; but Cambray had priests of every denomination, and pretended to adopt the opinions of each, until, at last, the base wretch proclaimed himself repented and contrite—a lamb gathered into the fold.

CHAPTER XVII.

Religion in the "lock-up."—The character of Cambray from a new point of view.

As stated in the preceding chapter, Cambray asked for and received ministers of every religious belief, and for the space of two days appeared to waver between the doctrines of each; at last he determined in favour of Catholicism, and affected to adopt all its rites; he did not, however, cease to hold interviews with the ministers of other churches, for his object, as will appear hereafter, was to interest all in his favour.

The Catholic priest who attended him in his cell, deceived by his false pretences of honesty, had frequently visited him as a friend previous to his arrest.

"Ah well, Cambray," said the young priest with much softness, "how do you do?—doubtless ill at ease and troubled in spirit, I come to offer you as much consolation in your present state as lies in my power. You and I were well known to each other at one time; I never thought it could have come to this. You greatly deceived me. But it would be cruel to reproach you in a moment like the present, far better to lead you on the road to repentance, and to awaken you to the voice of reconciliation with God."

"Ah Heaven," replied Cambray, "with all my heart; I am indeed ill and suffer much, but not to compare with the torments of my soul. I know full well, that, for me there is neither help nor the consolation of refuge in religion; mankind is now to me as nothing, God can only save me, could I but obtain his pardon; but there is one thing that troubles me greatly. Among so many religions of which I cannot tell one from the other, which is the best—how can a man in my circumstances, decide within an instant upon a matter of such great importance, without fear of mistake."

"Your moments are short and precious," said the young priest, "and you are entirely ignorant in the science of salvation, as Catholic priest and according to my belief, I must tell you in the presence of God and man, whom I take as witness of my sincerity and according to the founders of Christianity, that out of the Catholic and Apostolic Church of Rome there is no salvation. But as I have said your moments are short and precious—I could prove to you each of the doctrines of our religion, but is there time? The Saviour did not tell us to discuss and prove, but to believe and pray, it is not with contentious subtlety that we must walk in the way of truth, but with a humble submissive and trusting heart—faith is a grace to be obtained from Heaven by fervently asking at the sacrifice of passion and pride. If, therefore, you will throw yourself into the arms of the Catholic religion, say so, and I will devote myself wholly to your conversion—I will pour into your soul

the sweet consolations of holy writ—mayhap the words of the Saviour may move you, and the example of his life inspire you with horror.of the sins you are guilty of; do not despair, for the religion of Christ is one of love, of charity and of compassion, it pours forth the balm of consolation alike in the hospital, in the prison, in the cabin of the poor and in the palace of the rich, on the troubles of the virtuous and on the remorse of the contrite. Your crimes are no doubt great, but God is full of mercy—believe, weep and pray, and his heart will open to receive you."

These words pronounced with deep impressiveness had nearly softened the heart of the condemned, and in accents of grief, he cried out in a fit of passing repentance.

"Truly do I throw myself without delay into the arms of Divine mercy—I deplore my crimes and sincerely ask for pardon, but the time is so short—if people of virtue and influence would only interest themselves on my behalf—but, alas, human justice in condemning does not allow time for repentance. Do you think there would be any use in making the request?"

"Reckon not on that, for you may be deceived, and place yourself in a position of false security—perhaps it might be better for the salvation of your soul were death to remove you while repentance lasted, for the flesh is weak and the spirit strong in a nature as vitiated as thine. However, I will think of it. I will speak of it, and above all, I will regulate my conduct in accordance with the hopes I may entertain of your salvation."

The religion of Christ is touching and sublime, when it reveals to the unfortunate words of love and welcome, the mission of the priest noble and philanthropic, who visits even the cell of the condemned to administer peace and consolation, and the man who refuses it, must, indeed be devoid of heart, and totally incurable. But why does religion extend pardon when the law withholds it—the former recoils from blood, the latter desires it—the former offers salvation, the latter presents despair and death. The law then that establishes punishment by death is inhuman, or rather, I should say, almost impious; it deprives of existence, yet throws a doubting soul into eternity.

Pause ye Legislators of our country, is there no means of reforming the fallen, instead of annihilating them. True, executions are rare, but still the law permits them, and if the law is not enforced, it becomes dangerous, a pledge of impunity and an invitation to crime. The reprobate who contemplates a violation of the law, thinks only of the punishment with which his offences are threatened, and if he discovers that there is a means of escape, he easily assures himself of the probability.

"At last," said Cambray, (for we must return to our subject), "I flatter myself that you will think of some means by which my sentence may be commuted, I will see you to-morrow, for I have never been baptised, I believe."

"Yes, I will return to-morrow," said the priest. "Good bye—peace be with you, but remember that in three days you are to appear before the Eternal tribunal." He then left.

"I do not despair," said Cambray to Mathieu, who, during the entire interview described, spoke not a syllable. "If I can only interest the clergy in my favor, we are saved," and a leer of satisfaction and hope lit up his countenance, for as yet he was only half repentant and half triumphant.

"It takes a good color," said Mathieu, "it takes a good color."

CHAPTER XVIII.

A visit to the prison—Charland—The Condemned—Gillan the murderer—Exportation—Departure.

Some days after the Criminal Term 1837, we visited the prison, and the turnkey introduced us to the rooms occupied by the criminals, he was on his rounds to ascertain the safety of his prisoners, this he repeated three times during the night, at eight o'clock, at midnight and at four in the morning. Each storey of the prison is divided by a passage or corridor, on each side of which are the rooms occupied by the prisoners. Each room is about fifteen feet square and contained twelve or fifteen persons ; round these rooms which are used in common, are small cells, each of which serve as a sleeping apartment for two or three. As soon as the turnkey opens the door, the inmates range themselves in a semi-circle and answer to their names; those who have any thing to ask or any complaint to make profit by this occasion to lay their requests before the sheriff or jailer.

In the first room we visited, were such criminals as had been condemned to transportation ; there were thirteen in number, all in the flower of their age, the youngest being about twelve years of age, the eldest about twenty-five. It is hardly possible to imagine a more thievish and ill looking set than composed this party, nevertheless, they were all full of spirits and buffoonery, and joked gaily with each other on the difference of time each was condemned to endure in exile.

"I don't care," said a young lad of twelve or fifteen years, "I'm only in for seven years, I'm not like Johnny there, who has four times seven. Johnny will be a big boy when he gets back."

"Bah," said another, "there will be several of us, we'll find lots of amusement, never fear—we'll give lots of trouble too."

From this room, we passed into one in which were the old delinquents, the incorrigible vagabonds and permanent boarders of the king, whose lives cling to the prison as those of fishes do to the water or birds to the air. At their head was Charland a witty and lively hunchback, full of chatter, politeness and courtesy, his hair was lank and light in color, his complexion sallow, his figure squat and round, his head in his shoulders, his shoulders in his chest, and his chest in his stomach, just such a figure as Mr. Goulie paints us in his clown Gangrenet. Charland the redoubtable robber of the Plains of Abraham and cherished prisoner of the guardians, Charland sanguine and energetic whilst exercising his craft, but soft, jovial, amiable and full of fun when in jail,—lastly, Charland, thief and assassin—for the trade pleased him and he had no desire to change it.

"See here," said he, addressing the turnkey with an air of compassion and pointing out a young man who had nothing to cover him but a pair of torn trowsers, and whose bust was completely naked, "look at this poor child, look at him, could you not find him a shirt ? Know you not that the air is raw in this apartment."

"What did he do with the shirt given him yesterday ?" said the turnkey.

"I do not know—it was so bad—it came to pieces."

"Well, I'll think of it."

On leaving, we asked the turnkey why Charland appeared to take such an interest in the young man.

"It is," said he, "because Charland is *Brigadier*, that is to say, the senior of the room, and as such is the spokesman of the others. There is perhaps another reason, it often happens that the prisoners hide their clothes among themselves, in order to get others given them, so that they can change the first for tobacco and rum. For some days past Charland has been drunk from drinking liquor through an old pipe introduced through the gate by some friends without. It is nearly impossible to prevent communication with the people outside; every day we take from them instruments of every description, intended to pierce doors and walls, every day they are furnished with strong durable vestments, and yet they are always in rags,—they tear them among themselves. It is difficult to restrain these old troopers in crime, even the sewers and drains under the prison are to them attractive roads of escape. Mathieu once remained three days in the sewers beneath the city, amidst all the filth, visiting every nook to find an aperture by which to escape, until at last he was seized at one of the gratings, though not without deeply offending the nasal organs of the constables who discovered him."

From this room we went into one occupied by the unfortunate lunatics who ramble about our streets during the summer months, and whom the police keep from perishing during the intense severity of the winter by sending them to prison, in default of an asylum, an institution we do not yet possess. This assemblage was the most affecting and repulsive in the building, bearing upon it the impress of misery and degradation. The Baron Van Koring—the King of Scotland—Paddy the Chanter, and many other of our public notabilities were in this department.

Having inspected every quarter of the prison, one after the other, we at last arrived at the cell of the condemned. We perceived four men stretched on a miserable pallet all under sentence of death. Above them swung a solitary lamp which emitted a dim sepulchral light, and the pale yellow walls of the cell imparted their sickly hue to the care-worn features of the inmates—a soldier named Gillan, who had killed one of his companions, Cambray and Matthieu, for burglary, and Gagnon for the robbery of the Congregational Chapel.

The cell was so low, dark, and small that it seemed scarcely able to contain us. Before us lay the four figures of the inmates, so still that one might have believed them dead ; in perceiving us, however, Cambray raised himself and invited us to a seat on the bench beside him—the unique furniture of the apartment.

To our first question he made no answer except by lamentations upon the state of his health ; his manner was subdued as if by affliction, and he spoke in a low and broken tone of voice. He asked us what news there was respecting the circulation of his petition, and whether there was any probability of his obtaining his pardon. " It is not," said he " that I place much reliance upon the petition. I am quite resigned, and, as die we must, it matters little whether it comes sooner or later ; however, my friends have urged me to try it as a last chance, but there is little hope I believe."

" Have you heard anything about my sister ?" interrupted Mathieu, " I have just learned that she was found dead upon the ice. I know her disposition so well. She came from the country to ascertain how things went, and when she found me embroiled in this affair she poisoned herself."

" They have got up a petition for me in my parish, but it's quite useless ; by my faith, I'd as soon die now as not. Yesterday I saw a priest for about a quarter of an hour ; my affairs are well settled, and I am quite ready. I fear death no more than that," he added, puffing a cloud of smoke from his pipe, that unrolled itself in long spiral curves around his hideous person.

" Mathieu's a queer fellow," said Cambray, " he looks very simple, but he is *deep*—he looks far ahead of him. It's a singular truth that he steals from pure pleasure ; with him it is a passion, an impulse, dating from infancy ; and provided he steals, he concerns himself little about the booty." " You understand me Mathieu, is not that the case ?"

" No ! I don't know what you mean. It had never cost me a thought. I would not trouble myself to reason upon the matter."

" It is, as with the youngsters who are sentenced to transportation," said Cambray, " they are inborn thieves, and can follow no other occupation. They are a pretty set; the captain who is to conduct them to their place of destination will have occasion to be constantly on his guard. Amongst them all there are perhaps two or three possessed of sufficient courage to mutiny, but the cowardice of their companions (for thieves are nearly always cowards) will prevent anything of the kind ; for my part I would not enter into any compact with them under any circumstances ; they are too treacherous and too timid. Since I have been in prison, each time I attempted to escape I was betrayed, abandoned, even by those who had proposed the scheme. Ah, they have made me pay dearly for their treason ; they might organize a thousand conspiracies now, I would never join one of them. During the entire winter they have been making false keys to open all the doors, and yet they have not dared to make a single attempt to regain their freedom."

" O yes !" said Mathieu, " wooden keys; they accused me of making them, but without reason. I will not deny that I have frequently made them, but the merit of doing so on that occasion does not belong to me; there are many others who work at the trade besides myself. What a splendid exit we would have made last winter had not that infamous Provost sold the secret for a few favours ; his nature was too irresolute for a *coup de main* like that. The greater part of the prisoners we have with us are fit for nothing ; five or six had found the means of opening their doors, and of descending nightly into the yard ; at last they were discovered, chained, and thrown into cells ; they were not sufficiently punished for their cowardice. What ! descended every night to tremble in the yard, to gaze upon the moon, count the stars, without sufficient courage to scale the wall and escape; then return to their rooms chilled, with insipid excuses in their mouths, such as, ' it was too cold—we saw the guard—we did not know where to go to—to-morrow we will be braver.' Such cowardice merits the lock-up a do..en times over. I regret that I took no part in the scheme to desert, had I only known how this affair would have ended."

" If Waterworth," said Cambray " had not led me to hope that he would have united with me in that affair of Sivrac's, my trial would not have come off during the last Term. I would have taken care to have made myself ill. He played me a cruel trick, the infamous wretch Waterworth ; he's the most abject being within the prison walls."

" Yes, the accursed," added Mathieu, " he it was who got us into this scrape, but the devil will broil him for that trick."

" But Waterworth says," said I to Cambray " that it was you who first offered to turn king's evidence."

" No, no, no, it was proposed to me, but I would not ; if Waterworth betrayed us, it is because he has no conscience, he has not the bump of honesty, and so Dr. B—— told him a few months ago. Waterworth has no excuse ; he was actuated by wickedness, by fear ; he ought to be hung twenty times over. To make believe that he is innocent he represents himself as a coward; yes, he is a coward, and one of the vilest rascals into the bargain ; there was no fear of his compromising Norris and the others."

" I do not blame him," said Mathieu, " but he should not have put us in their stead ; that was not well done, that. Do you know it's dangerous to take the evidence of such as we are ; it should not be done ; to escape six months' imprisonment we could say anything. Waterworth had better leave Quebec, his days are not insured to him here ; we have associates who will avenge our fate."

" Nobody will speak to him," said Cambray, " he will never be received anywhere, the traitor. · Ah ! if I could only meet him, I'd—yes— but I do not wish to see him—no, I would do him no injury."

It would be necessary to have heard the accents in which these words were delivered, and to have seen the expression that accompanied them ; to understand and appreciate the full force of their hidden strength.

" I would not wish to be in his place," added Cambray, " though it is very hard to be condemned to die for having committed theft only. In the United States they hang only for murder, and it seems to me much more rational; the best punishment is transportation. Penitentiaries do not inspire much terror, but transportation, ah, it is desolate indeed; a man loves his native country for ever. The court has adopted a wise measure in transporting all the young thieves; it saves them from the gallows and frightens the rest. You will soon see brigandage on the decrease!"

" But, I think transportation should be the uniform punishment imposed by law, a commutation of sentence has not the same effect."

"For a man who walks on the edge of a precipice, ordinary danger is of no account, it leaves no impression on their minds. To the criminal condemned to death, exportation offers a consolation, a plank of salvation. Confined in his cell, cast down in despair, awaiting with horror the hour of the scaffold approaching, the knell to eternity—the door opens, he trembles in every limb, but no, he is assured of life, and falls joyously upon his pallet—he will not die on the scaffold—how sweet the transition—he is the happiest of criminals; exile presents nothing frightful to him who has been face to face with death."

"Cambray!" said the turnkey, "you saw a priest yesterday; they say that you have been converted, that you have turned Catholic, that you have been baptised."

"Yes, it is true to a certain extent. Oh! I do not know yet, it is not quite settled—these things require time—I am not yet decided—I have still doubts!"

" Ah, Cambray," said Mathieu, "do not speak in that way in the hour you have come to; is it possible you possess such sentiments?"

"Mathieu! I know what I've done, and what I have to do; mind your own affairs, or it will be I who will teach you. With me it was not to change a faith, but to choose one. I think, however, I would have believed in God had I reflected upon the subject."

" There are few who do not believe," observed Mathieu, "but people like us never think of him. Waterworth has often said to me, 'look here, Mathieu, after we are dead everything will be dead to us—take your course and fear nothing.' The miserable wretch, see what he has brought us to."

During this gabble between Cambray and Mathieu, Gagnon, remained perfectly quiet and passive, holding a book (the lives of Martyrs) in his hand, reading from time to time a few lines and casting side-long glances at us; he was silent, pensive, impatient of conversation, and appeared desirous of seeing our visit abridged. There was nothing in the appearance of this man to indicate the injustice of his sentence; on the contrary, the gallows and he appeared made for each other. But amidst these vile wretches how great was the contrast in favour of Gillan the murderer. Gillan raising his hands to heaven, deeply moved in spirit, rolling in mental agony upon his couch, striking his breast, his eyes filling with tears, his breath choking with sighs and remorse, Gillan alone indicated true fervent grief; alone was able to say "I am innocent." When we spoke to him " Yes," said he " I am a murderer, the murderer of my best friend. I was drunk, exasperated, furious; we were on the same guard, without a light, unknown to each other, I was unconscious of what I was doing. A knife fell into my hand and I struck—killed my best friend. Oh! what misfortune, what misfortune! To live in a cell with felons, and die with them in three days time. It is horrible, horrible. Oh! accursed drink, to me you have been fatal indeed."

The next day Cambray, Gillan, and Mathieu were informed that their sentence of death had been commuted to one of transportation, and that in two months they would accompany the others to new South Wales. From that moment there was nothing further of conversion. Mathieu and several others attempted to make their escape by a sewer. Cambray tried to make himself sick by swallowing tobacco, but the visiting physician divining his object, recommended a sea voyage to re-establish his health. At last, on the 29th of May, 1837, about ten o'clock in the morning, thirty-nine criminals, chained two and two, left the prison. Cambray and Mathieu at their head. Arriving beneath the gibbet, they simultaneously burst forth in loud and repeated hurrahs, and then marched joyously towards the gate, saluting this one and calling to that, like old soldiers leaving for the army. They were placed on board the brig Ceres, Captain Squire commanding, and that evening they set sail for the Antipodes.

THE END.

www.ingramcontent.com/pod-product-compliance
Lightning Source LLC
Chambersburg PA
CBHW032033090426
42733CB00031B/1193